The Best
Stage Scenes
of 1993

Smith and Kraus *Books For Actors*
THE MONOLOGUE SERIES
> The Best Men's/Women's Stage Monologues of 1993
> The Best Men's/Women's Stage Monologues of 1992
> The Best Men's/Women's Stage Monologues of 1991
> The Best Men's/Women's Stage Monologues of 1990
> One Hundred Men's/Women's Stage Monologues from the 1980's
> 2 Minutes and Under: Character Monologues for Actors
> Street Talk: Character Monologues for Actors
> Uptown: Character Monologues for Actors
> Monologues from Contemporary Literature: Volume I
> Monologues from Classic Plays

FESTIVAL MONOLOGUE SERIES
> The Great Monologues from the Humana Festival
> The Great Monologues from the EST Marathon
> The Great Monologues from the Women's Project
> The Great Monologues from the Mark Taper Forum

YOUNG ACTORS SERIES
> Great Scenes and Monologues for Children
> New Plays from A.C.T.'s Young Conservatory
> Great Scenes for Young Actors from the Stage
> Great Monologues for Young Actors

SCENE STUDY SERIES
> Scenes From Classic Plays 468 B.C. to 1970 A.D.
> The Best Stage Scenes of 1993
> The Best Stage Scenes of 1992
> The Best Stage Scenes for Men/Women from the 1980's

PLAYS FOR ACTORS SERIES
> Romulus Linney: 17 Short Plays
> Eric Overmyer: Collected Plays
> Lanford Wilson: 21 Short Plays
> William Mastrosimone: Collected Plays
> Horton Foote: 4 New Plays
> Israel Horovitz: 17 Short Plays

GREAT TRANSLATION FOR ACTORS SERIES
> The Wood Demon by Anton Chekhov

OTHER BOOKS IN OUR COLLECTION
> Humana Festival '93: The Complete Plays
> The Actor's Chekhov
> Women Playwrights: The Best Plays of 1992
> Kiss and Tell: Restoration Scenes, Monologues, & History
> Cold Readings: Some Do's and Don'ts for Actors at Auditions

If you require pre-publication information about upcoming Smith and Kraus monologues collections, scene collections, play anthologies, advanced acting books, and books for young actors, you may receive our semi-annual catalogue, free of charge, by sending your name and address to *Smith and Kraus Catalogue, P.O. Box 10, Newbury, VT 05051. (800) 862 5423 FAX (802) 866 5346*

The Best
Stage Scenes
of 1993

edited by Jocelyn A. Beard

The Scene Study Series

SK
A Smith and Kraus Book

Published by Smith and Kraus, Inc.
Newbury, Vermont
Copyright © 1993 by Smith and Kraus, Inc.

COVER AND TEXT DESIGN BY JULIA HILL
Manufactured in the United States of America

First Edition: January 1994
10 9 8 7 6 5 4 3 2 1

ISSN 1067-3253 Scene Study Series
ISBN 1-880399-44-X

NOTE: These scenes are intended to be used for audition and class study; permission is not required to use the material for those purposes. However, if there is a paid performance of any of the scenes included in this book, please refer to the permissions acknowledgment pages to locate the source who can grant permission for public performance.

*I would like to dedicate this book to George Puello,
Associate Producer at the Westchester Broadway Theatre,
who taught me a lot of what I really needed to know.*

CONTENTS

O   O   O

SCENES FOR WOMEN

SCENES FOR MEN

Foreword

Whew! What a season! To say that I'm emotionally drained after reading the plays enclosed in this volume would be at the very least an understatement. The word is: Dark. The plays of the 1993 season are very dark; some delightfully and some devastatingly. AIDS, cancer, rape, child abuse, torture—you name it, many of the plays of 1993 deal with the most painful issues in human history. I could detail some of them here for you in a fashion typical of editors' forewords, but I will instead urge you to read as many of these plays as you are able, for they tell stories of profound importance, and deserve your undivided attention—not just as actors, but as residents of planet Earth.

The scenes that I have collected for you will provide quite an array of creative possibilities, and should inspire you to increase your range. There are no simple roles in this book. Be prepared to encounter some extremely complex characters. Characters like the mother in *Snakebit* who fears that she has given her daughter AIDS, or the adult children of Nazis who torment themselves over the deeds of their fathers in *Born Guilty*, or men waiting for freedom or death in *Someone Who'll Watch Over Me*. These are amazing tales peopled by fascinating individuals inviting you to share—if only for a moment or two—their breath. I encourage you, the actor, to join in their stories and make them your own.

Break a leg!

Jocelyn A. Beard
Patterson, NY
December 1993

Introduction

You are holding much more than the best new tool for theatre training. *The Best Stage Scenes of 1993* can open the world for you as seen through the eyes of our most talented contemporary playwrights. If scenes are moments in time which allow us to explore character and relationships, the scenes in this volume are drawn from plays that paint for us an extraordinary portrait of our time. While our focused study of the elements of drama remains a constant, each year the stage view of our world evolves or changes completely. Here we have the benefit of some remarkable new scene work , as well as a unique window to that world.

The range of work represented here reflects a 1993 reality that is both healthy and exciting: the established regionalism of American theatre. These playwrights have found artistic homes throughout the country, where theatres help to nurture new plays through the process of development and production. As a result, we have a rich body of material that covers a spectrum of dramatic style and structure. Issues and ideas are illuminated from various perspectives. Locations take us all over the map, from the Minnesota ice hut in Kevin Kling's *The Ice Fishing Play* to the sidewheeler on the Mississippi River of Val Smith's *The Gamblers*; from Bensonhurst, Brooklyn in Frank Pugliese's *Aven'u Boys* to *Stanton's Garage*, Joan Ackermann's quintessential stop on the way to and from her very own "mainstream" America. And all of these scenes are abundantly populated with a diverse community of characters that will exercise, develop, and challenge the skills of actors and directors on every level. So, whether you are looking for a new scene to sink your teeth into, or you just want to listen to the voices of some of our country's best storytellers, this collection provides an exceptional opportunity.

—Louis Tyrrell
  Artistic Director, Pope Theatre Company
  Manalapan, FL

Scenes
For Men and Women

BORN GUILTY
by Ari Roth

Dramatic / 1 Man, 1 Woman
 Brigitte & Rainer: brother and sister; the children of a Nazi
  war criminal, 40-50

The Setting: Germany, the present

When Brigitte and Rainer are interviewed by Peter Sichrovsky for
his book on the children of Nazis, they reveal painful emotional
wounds that will never be healed.

O   O   O

(*Lights up on Rainer and Brigitte. The place is an artist's pig-
sty.*)

RAINER: What? You don't like what I've done with the living
room?

BRIGITTE: You mean, turn it into a scrap heap?

RAINER: Typical. That is a typical, Christian Democratic response!

[**PETER:** (*To audience.*) I call them . . . "THE SEPARABLES."]

BRIGITTE: Tell me, why do you insist on labeling people?

RAINER: I have no idea what you mean by "labeling!"
(*Muttering.*) Lousy upper-middle-class, wine-and-cheese . . .

BRIGITTE: (*To Peter.*) See what I mean?

[**PETER:** (*To audience.*) This is the first time they've seen each
other in three years. I thought it might make for a good story.
You know, "Bridging the gulf . . . ?"]

RAINER: Let's first agree on terminology. Our father was – what?

BRIGITTE: He was a high-ranking –

RAINER: PUPPET, maybe?

BRIGITTE: "*Offizier.*"

RAINER: "*Offizier.*"

[**PETER:** (*To audience.*) And as with any good "Bridging-the-
Gulf" saga, we have your obligatory "Car Crash."]

RAINER: He and his fellow "*Offizierin des Generalstabs*"
established whatever measures necessary to create
LEBENSRAUM for the claustrophobic-at-heart.

[**PETER:** (*To audience.*) Or in this case, "*Train Wreck.*"]

RAINER: (*Overlapping.*) For them, war was sport.

BRIGITTE: War was war.

RAINER: Colored pins on a map.

[**PETER:** (*To audience.*) Two locomotives hurtling down the same track . . .]

RAINER: Victory, the equivalent of a business deal.

BRIGITTE: Tell us, little brother, what would you know of "Victory," much less a successful "business deal?"

RAINER: Certainly not as much as your Heinrich. Shall we begin again? I've taken the liberty of arranging all papers in chronological order, beginning with memberships, medals. All to be hung in my next work –

BRIGITTE: He no longer believes in the WASTE-BASKET!

RAINER: (*Overlapping.*) "Familial Abstractions: Shrine to this family's failure."

BRIGITTE: Only yours.

RAINER: (*To Peter.*) You know, she married one. A banker. Just like the old –

BRIGITTE: Your FATHER provided for you, Rainer, just as Heinrich and I have offered to –

RAINER: To what? Buy me out?

BRIGITTE: Not you. This house. Buy this house.

RAINER: This house is not for sale, thank you. It is a work in progress. A rotting, crumbling, life-size composition.

BRIGITTE: Such stupidity. And for what? Did he ever once strike you?

RAINER: He never touched me!

BRIGITTE: Exactly. He wiped the chocolate off your mouth, took you out into the garden, and played soccer. Soccer for hours. Father and son.

RAINER: "*RAINER KOMM! PLAY FOOTBALL!*"

BRIGITTE: As it should be!

RAINER: "DON'T YOU WANT TO BE LIKE ALL THE OTHER BOYS!"

BRIGITTE: He was your Ideal!

RAINER: He was our Fraud! Who knows what other frauds he was playing simultaneously? What other disguises!? Soccer with a smile: That was mine. Never mind my concerns, only bring HIM joy!

BRIGITTE: Poor Rainer.

RAINER: One word, one question, Mother would launch into the litany: *"HASN'T HE BEEN THROUGH ENOUGH!? SIX YEARS OF WAR, FOUR YEARS OF PRISON . . . SIX YEARS OF WAR, FOUR YEARS OF PRISON . . . "* He'd just sit there listening like a stuffed doll. *"WASSER . . . EIN GLAS . . . BITTE, RAINER!"*

BRIGITTE: Stop it.

RAINER: "Get your own water, you old fart!"

BRIGITTE: I will not have you talk this way.

RAINER: That's what *I'd* tell him.

BRIGITTE: (*To Peter.*) Our father believed in a future. A promising, respectable future, whereas he, he only wallows in shame. In DUST BALLS.

RAINER: (*Holding up the collection of war papers.*) For two hundred years the men in this family have handed down a tradition of unconditional obedience and surrender! I, thank God, am BREAKING that chain!

BRIGITTE: By sponging off father?

RAINER: (*Into the tape recorder.*) I am the first NON-MILITARIST in this family in over two hundred –

BRIGITTE: Every Mao tract you bought was paid for by his bank. Every cigarette came straight out of his pocket. WHAT REBELLION, RAINER? You've never worked! You've never shown. YOU ARE THE OFFSPRING OF GERMAN OFFICERS, and not your slumming on some kibbutz nor your ravings about fascism, are EVER GOING TO CHANGE THAT!
(*To audience.*)
He tried converting – You should have seen. Star of David around his neck. Later, of course, a Palestinian shawl. Oh, and the women! Those last surviving hippies of the decade smoking pot, straggling out of his room in their panties with nothing on top.

RAINER: You sound jealous.

BRIGITTE: Jealous? You, the laughing stock, and I sound jealous? Just because I didn't turn myself into a freak show? Some sex machine? I had friends.

RAINER: Sure, everyone wants to fuck the daughter of a late-great Nazi.

BRIGITTE: Stop it.

[**PETER:** (*To audience.*) Did they? Could that be right?]

BRIGITTE: (*Back to Rainer.*) You can attack me all you like, but I will not have you attack him!

RAINER: I AM NOT ATTACKING!

[PETER: Did I really want to "fuck the daughters of . . . "]

RAINER: I AM ADMITTING! YES, I'VE DONE MY SHARE OF IDIOTIC DEEDS! YES, I'VE WORN MY SHARE OF IDIOTIC CLOTHES. BUT NOT OUT OF SPITE!

[PETER: (*To audience.*) I didn't like the way he put that . . .]

RAINER: ALL I WANTED WAS A SIMPLE EXPLANATION! A SIMPLE MEANING!

BRIGITTE: There is NO "MEANING," RAINER! There is no "EXPLANATION." You keep wanting to reduce everything! Yes, we lost the war. Yes, this family felt it more than most. We started it, after all! We *dreamed* it. No it easy wasn't dragging ourselves up from the abyss, but we did it. We mended. Now we need to talk about this house. About who is going to live in it. Not just DIE in it. So that it might stand for a new generation.

RAINER: And which generation did you have in mind? Ours?

BRIGITTE: Yes. Why not let the children make a go of it?

RAINER: Ah, the children . . .

BRIGITTE: Rainer.

RAINER: Heinrich still won't give you any children?

BRIGITTE: Heinrich is not the issue here. I think it might be a good idea for you to move on, that's all.

RAINER: When exactly are we planning on having this "new generation," Brigitte? You are forty-two years old.

BRIGITTE: Anything else?

RAINER: Is it that you want to but you can't?

BRIGITTE: (*To Peter.*) . . . Could you stop the tape for a minute?

RAINER: So that's it?

BRIGITTE: How much do you want? Here's my checkbook.

RAINER: "*Fraulein Future* lays a goose egg?"

BRIGITTE: I WILL NOT HAVE YOU DRAG ME DOWN INTO THE MUD WITH YOU!!!

RAINER: Admit it.

BRIGITTE: I did not come here for this.

RAINER: Everything that goes in becomes poisoned.

BRIGITTE: I don't know you.

RAINER: Just say it. Say the truth.

BRIGITTE: Last chance! Name your price!

RAINER: I know what it's like.

BRIGITTE: (*To Peter.*) I ASKED YOU TO TURN THAT THING OFF!

RAINER: I can help you!

BRIGITTE: NO. YOU CAN'T! YOU CANNOT HELP ME!

(*To Peter.*)

I would like my release form back, thank you! My father was a good father.

THE BUTCHER'S DAUGHTER
by Wendy Kesselman

Dramatic / 1 Man, 1 Woman
>Olympe de Gouges: a playwright, pamphleteer and advocate
>of human rights during the French Revolution, 20-30
>Le Franc De Pompignan: the man she believes to be her
>father, 40-50

The Setting: Paris, just before the Revolution of 1789

Olympe has made her way to Paris where she hopes to become a playwright. When she has completed her first play, she gathers up enough courage to confront the man rumored to be her father.

O   O   O

(*Le Franc de Pompignan's Paris apartment. Olympe and the elegantly attired Le Franc de Pompignan stand facing each other.*)

LE FRANC DE POMPIGNAN: Who let you in?
(*Moving past her toward the door.*)
I told them never to –

OLYMPE: (*Stepping in front of him.*) You know me then? Monsieur Le Franc de Pompignan?

LE FRANC DE POMPIGNAN: (*After a pause.*) You've changed, of course. From the scruffy ragamuffin constantly being booted out the chateau gate in Montauban.

OLYMPE: (*Smiling.*) Yes. I've changed.

LE FRANC DE POMPIGNAN: You've become – how shall I put it? A lady.
(*He smiles just slightly.*)
Of sorts.
(*Olympe is silent.*)
Well. Now that you're here, I suppose I can't boot you out again.
(*Turning to Olympe.*)
What can I do for you? Hm?

(*Silence.*)

How may I help you? Presuming of course, that you need help. You do need help, don't you? I mean . . . you do want something of me.

OLYMPE: I – I sent you my manuscript. My play.

LE FRANC DE POMPIGNAN: (*After a moment, his hand just grazing an unbound manuscript on the table before him.*) Yes. I have it right here.

OLYMPE: Have you read it?

LE FRANC DE POMPIGNAN: (*Smiling slightly.*) Well, shall we say, I began. I tried.

(*Pausing, as she stares at him.*)

If I may ask again, how may I be of assistance? What exactly do you want? Do you need money? Clothes? Something to eat perhaps? You look like you need –

OLYMPE: (*Overlapping.*) To write. I want to write.

LE FRANC DE POMPIGNAN: Ah. To write. Yes. Of course.

(*A pause.*)

Well, you have written –

(*His finger lightly tapping her play.*)

This.

OLYMPE: In the right way. To be able to tell what I see every day, every hour. I see things. Everywhere I go. Women. Children. Beggars. Here in Paris. At home in Montauban. People in poverty. Despair. People I reach out my hand to. People I can touch. A girl running, clutching a loaf of bread. A stone flying after her. I want to write about her. Tell her story.

(*Le Franc laughs.*)

LE FRANC DE POMPIGNAN: Well go ahead, my dear. By all means. Tell all their stories. It really doesn't concern me.

OLYMPE: You read me something once – something that rhymed – in a cloud-blue room. I've never forgotten.

(*Coming closer to Le Franc.*)

Please. Show me. Teach me how. I want to – I need to learn.

(*A pause.*)

I brought you something. It belongs to you.

(*Gently, she hands him the feather pen.*)

LE FRANC DE POMPIGNAN: (*Turning the pen about slowly.*) Show you what exactly?

OLYMPE: It's easy for you. I know that. You write poetry. Plays.

LE FRANC DE POMPIGNAN: Nothing is easy. For anyone. How long did it take you to write –

(*He lifts a corner of the manuscript.*)

This? For example.

OLYMPE: Forty-eight hours.

LE FRANC DE POMPIGNAN: Forty-eight hours! Indeed.

(*He chuckles.*)

Well, we can't all have what we want in this life, my dear. I can't help you to write. No one can. You simply haven't got it in you. (*Flipping through the pages of the unbound manuscript.*)

You can't even write French, my dear child. I only wish you could.

(*Olympe grabs the first page of her script, begins reading it aloud.*)

OLYMPE: (*Stumbling over the words.*) "Vir-Virtue Rewarded." Scene One. Vassent speaks: "Oh! My daughter! Oh! My blood!" The Cho-Chorus speaks: "What joy, what hap-happiness to be – be her fa-father –"

LE FRANC DE POMPIGNAN: (*Cutting in.*) You see, my dear? You can hardly even speak the language. How can you expect to write a full length play? You can't spell. You have no grammar. You write in a barely legible hand. There are mistakes on every page, in every sentence – from beginning to end! Please do me the honor of making this the last time you send me anything you have written. There's not a line in here that's memorable.

(*Looking down at the play. Quiet.*)

This is . . . at best . . . embarrassing.

OLYMPE: (*Soft.*) You could have helped me. Sent me to school. (*Softer yet.*) You could have taught me.

LE FRANC DE POMPIGNAN: Let's not be absurd.

OLYMPE: (*Coming close and touching the feather pen in his hand.*) You could teach me now.

LE FRANC DE POMPIGNAN: Forty eight hours! Amazing!

(*He laughs aloud.*) Only someone with genius could possibly –

OLYMPE: (*Interrupting.*) I have genius.

LE FRANC DE POMPIGNAN: Ah! You have genius.

(*Slapping her play.*) That's hilarious. And where, may I ask, does your genius come from?

OLYMPE: You. (*As Le Franc steps back.*)
I get it from you. You're my –

LE FRANC DE POMPIGNAN: (*Tossing the unbound pages of her play in the air.*) That's a lie! Just village talk. Forget it.

OLYMPE: I can't.

LE FRANC DE POMPIGNAN: You must! Stay in your place. Be who you are. Don't think you can be anyone but who you are. A butcher's daughter from Montauban! You'll never be anything else. (*Quiet.*)
You should have stayed in Montauban. (*He pauses.*) But you're here now. You found your way to the Capital. You have beauty, just like your mother. . . even as a child. You have admirers. What more do you want? Live the gallant life, Olympe. Stay out of the theatre. And out of politics, too. It's no place for a woman these days. (*He looks at her.*) I can give you no better help than that. (*Olympe is silent, looking down.*) And now, if I may suggest. . . My wife, fortunately, is away today, but if she were ever to know – if she were ever even to guess – (*He pauses.*) Your very name – (*He stops.*)

OLYMPE: (*After a moment.*) I may not come again?

LE FRANC DE POMPIGNAN: From now on this house must be closed to you.
(*He steps forward, lightly grazes her hand with his lips. Olympe bends down, picks up the scattered pages of her play. She stands still, hesitating.*)

OLYMPE: I just wanted to say – I didn't mean – I never thought – In no way have I ever wanted to embarrass you, (*A pause.*) Monsieur Le Marquis. An embarrassment. That's the last thing I want to be. (*He is silent. She looks down at the play in her hand.*) I only thought – I only hoped you might – (*She looks up. Le Franc's face remains impenetrable.*) No. (*Still silence.*) Well then. (*She looks at him, curtseys slightly. She smiles. His face does not change. She turns to go, stops, turns back.*) You were right. There is something I came here for. Something I didn't know myself.

LE FRANC DE POMPIGNAN: (*Wary.*) What is that?

OLYMPE: A word. One word.

LE FRANC DE POMPIGNAN: Ah. (*A pause.*) Which one? (*Olympe is silent.*) Hurry. I have an appointment.

OLYMPE: (*Stepping forward.*) You know the one. (*As Le Franc* *moves back.*) I'm too intense aren't I? Just like I was outside the chateau gate in Montauban.

LE FRANC DE POMPIGNAN: My appointment. Please.

OLYMPE: My word. Please. (*They stand silent, facing each other.*) Do you think I can't hear it humming in your head? It hums in mine. It never stops. It's who I am. What you made me. The one word that says I belong to you.

LE FRANC DE POMPIGNAN: (*Turning away.*) You never belonged to me.

OLYMPE: (*Grabs hold of his jacket.*) Please. Tell me. Why I'm not a human being with thoughts and feelings the same as you. Why I'm worthless. Why I have no rights of my own. You have to say it. You must!

LE FRANC DE POMPIGNAN: I don't have to say anything. Don't try to manipulate me. (*Trying to shake her off.*) Get off, I tell you! What do you want from me? Money? Land? My name perhaps? You'll never get it. As a girl – a girl child – a – (*Snorting.*)
You don't even exist. You're not entitled to anything!

OLYMPE: I don't want anything! Only the word that belongs to me. The word you were about to say. I won't leave until you do.

LE FRANC DE POMPIGNAN: (*Pulling her across the floor with him.*) You'll leave. I'll make you leave.

OLYMPE: (*Clinging to him.*) You'll have to boot me out, Monsieur Le Franc de Pompignan – just like in Montauban. Only we're in Paris now and everyone will see, everyone will know.

LE FRANC DE POMPIGNAN: You wouldn't dare, little girl child! Little – (*He stops. Soft, seductive.*) All right. You want me to say it? I'll say it. I'll say it for you.
(*Almost spitting out the word.*) Bastard! Bastard! Little girl baby who should never have been born. Good only to be thrown away. Out of my sight. (*Dragging her to the door.*) Little bitch. Little bastard bitch.
(*Kicking her away from him. Exhausted.*)
There. Satisfied? Are you satisfied now?

OLYMPE: (*She picks herself up, stands very straight, very tall, holding the pages of her script to her breast. In tears. Smiling.*) Yes. (*She goes out.*)

CHRISTCHILD
by J. e Franklin

Serio-Comic / 1 Man, 1 Woman
 Tom: a boy with a chip on his shoulder, 15
 Gertie: an ancient conjurer and healer, 80s

The Setting: rural Texas during the Roosevelt years

When Tom encounters Gertie, the local wise woman, she tells him of the mysterious occurrences at his birth. The two then witness what may or may not be a divine visitation.

GERTIE: Awww . . . coo-ca-roo! What a pretty birrrd! Gonna git me one-a them pretty feathers for my Stetson-hat? Hee-heee . . . . where your girlfriend at? I hear you over here sometime just a-waking me up 'fore daylight. Why'n you come on over in my yard? My hens ain't laying like they used'ta . . . hee-heee. He shore is a fine one, Tommy. Where you get him?
TOM: He used to be an Easter chick. Theirs died . . . mine didn't.
GERTIE: Praise God! See this feather in my hat . . . ?
(She points to her hat.)
H'it tell me everything I wanna know.
(Tom is visibly uneasy.)
GERTIE: H'it say your baby brother gonna be all right. And h'it say your little heart is hurting like a so'.
TOM: I'm busy now, Miss Gertie.
GERTIE: I got business with you, battle-boy. Miss Gertie don't blame you for being scared-a me. They done scandalized my name so. I 'spects that grizzly bear they got at that carnival be scared-a me, too.
TOM: I ain't scared-a no grizzly bear and I ain't scared-a you, neither.
GERTIE: Oh, I knows you ain't scared-a nothing. Them Westmorelands knows it, too . . . hee-heee. I mean you whupped them good! Where's the jawbone-a that ass you was using?

TOM: (*Loosening up with a grin.*) It was just a stick.

GERTIE: You done 'em 'zackly right. Old Pootie, he was the ring'tail leader. That's the one d'rapped his britches to me and showed me the eclipse-a his moon. And my lips is sealed, honey. If'n them Westmorelands or anybody hear-tell you ran from a little, old po' lady like me, h'it won't be me what told 'em . . . naw-sir! My lips is sealed!

TOM: I ain't scared-a you, Miss Gertie.

GERTIE: (*A cunning smile plays on her cherubic face.*) God bless your heart, honey. Miss Gertie don't care 'bouts the rest-a these young'uns running from her, but h'it hurt me to my heart for you to do it 'cause Miss Gertie love you, honey.

TOM: Who, me?

GERTIE: God knows I do! Ever' since the day I delivered you into this world. I wanted to be your godmammy but they wouldn't have me.

TOM: *You* delivered me?!

GERTIE: Didn't your momma and pappy tell you h'it was me delivered you?

TOM: N'om, they ain't told me nothing.

GERTIE: I don't do that mid-wifin' no mo' but I 'members the day you was born, I do! The sun stood still in the heaven . . . ducks was runnin' and hollerin' and that light shining 'round you was bright as that sun up there . . .

TOM: A light?!

GERTIE: You was born with a veil!

TOM: Who, me?!

GERTIE: Miss Gertie was right there, honey! I was born with a veil, too . . . You and me is God's chilluns!

TOM: Who? I ain't none-a His child.

GERTIE: Yes you is, too, honey! And I loves you good as God do!

TOM: Shoot, God don't even love me.

GERTIE: Who dat say dat?! Who dat say He don't?!

TOM: When he ever loved me?

GERTIE: (*Reverting to the childlike.*) When? When the "wind" broke-wind . . . hee-heee. Honey, God love you in the beginning and the end.

TOM: So why he make me have six fingers?

GERTIE: . . . Six is a perfect number . . . H'it's the first number made out-a its own parts. Oh, I knows my numbers, honey

. . . the sixth, the third and the half. What is that? Ain't it one, two, three? Ain't that the Trinity? Don't tell me h'it ain't. Me and the Master, we looks beyond your faults and sees your needs . . . and we loves you, honey . . .

(*Gertie jumps back, seeing some force Tom can't see. The boy backs off apprehensively.*)

Sa-Kacha ma-ganzi! Do, Jesus! Sa-kachamaganzi!

TOM: What?! What you saying?! What you doing?!

(*Gertie's eyes trace a path from the ground heavenward.*)

GERTIE: Yon' it go, honey! H'it just got lifted up! Your bird see it! Do, Jesus!

TOM: Where?! Where?!

(*The rooster crows a medley of alleluiahs.*)

GERTIE: Don't you see it?! Your bird see it!

TOM: (*Frightened and straining.*) I don't see nothing!

GERTIE: Shore you can, honey! If anybody can see it, h'it'll be you! Look with the eyes of the eagle! Look! H'it's going off . . . ! Your bird see it! Look yonder!

TOM: I see it! I see Him, Miss Gertie!

GERTIE: Do, Jesus!

TOM: He look kind-a sad.

GERTIE: Yes . . . yes! What else you see?

TOM: His eyes is on fire!

GERTIE: That's the one, honey! That's Him, all right!

TOM: He going away now!

GERTIE: Yeah, but you seen Him!

TOM: I did see Him, Miss Gertie . . . I really did!

GERTIE: Shore you did, honey! You just seen the Holy Ghost! Blessed lamb! I told ya' you was the one! You gonna deliver your family!

(*Gertie suddenly seizes Tom's awed face in her hands.*)

TOM: Help me, Miss Gertie!

GERTIE: Bend on down to me, honey. Blessed lamb! Lord-God-A'mighty, bless your Christchild! Black sheep your lamb, too Lord. Bless him Father!

(*Gertie plants three kisses on each of Tom's eyes before releasing the stunned boy, and then she chants over him.*)

 I see black boy swing from the tree
 His feets don't touch the ground
 He lift his face and call on the Lord

to come and cut him down.

Deliver him, Lord! Deliver him! Deliver him!

Saka chema-ganzi . . . !

(*Gertie reaches into her apron pocket, takes out something, and presses it into Tom's hand.*)

GERTIE: This is for you, honey . . . joog you a hole in it and wear it 'round your neck. The gates-a hell won't prevail again' you. (*Tom stares down into his hand at the shiny dime which Gertie has left there. Gertie lays her hand on Tom and a current passes through her. She leaves the kneeling Tom stunned and mesmerized by the coin . . . and then he looks heavenward in awe.*)

Saka-chema-ganzi!

DICK'S ISLAND
by Caroline Cromelin & Ginger Donelson

Serio-Comic / 1 Man, 1 Woman
Nova & Jock: a married couple plotting to steal an island, 30s

The Setting: Dick's Island off the coast of Georgia, the present

On the eve of their patriarch's birthday, Nova reveals that she desires the family's island home for the purpose of turning it into a "Gone With The Wind" theme park.

O   O   O

(Nova Nuggett enters with cigarette and arranges herself seductively in bed, watching a videotape of "Gone With the Wind.")
NOVA: *(Calling.)* Come on, Jock. They're already at Tara! *(Lighting a cigarette.)* Jock! You don't want to miss the Tarleton twins. They're your favorites.
(Jock Nuggett enters, all attention on the television.)
JOCK: Now those two boys are my idea of real Southern manhood. They're good looking, well spoken, and they know how to dress.
NOVA: They say that that one there –
JOCK: George Reeves?
NOVA: Was a pansy.
JOCK: Come on, Nova, he played Superman.
NOVA: Speaking of Superman. *(She pats bed suggestively.)*
JOCK: Look at the way Scarlett flirts with those two. Ah! There goes that little eyebrow. Whenever she does that, men melt. *(Nova blows a stream of smoke seductively at Jock.)* Nova, I though you gave up smoking?
NOVA: I did, but not in bed.
JOCK: Honey, did you do something to your hair?
NOVA: I want it to be as blond as possible for the pig roast tonight. Reporters from England are going to be there.
JOCK: Nova, when are you going to stop denying your red highlights?

NOVA: Never. I resent being a red head. Always treated like cotton candy on a stick. I guess that's one more thing on which we don't see eye to eye.

JOCK: Come on, Nova. I do everything you ask. I even had that vasectomy you insisted on, on our wedding day.

NOVA: That was like putting a choke chain on a caterpillar. Wait a minute. Freeze frame. Right there. What do you see?

JOCK: Scarlett running away from Tara.

NOVA: Tara. Do you remember we were watching this one night back in Tarboro, and you promised me, "Babe, I'm gonna buy you a house just like that, just like Tara, down on Dick's." And what are we living in now? A split-level beach-front ranch-house condo. Not Tara. You lied to me. You married me under false pretenses.

JOCK: Come on, Nova. You know I'm trying to buy you Arcadia. It's my fondest dream to see you standing among those columns as mistress of our own plantation –

NOVA: Arcadia. That place is a beautiful expanse of unspoiled virgin land, just crying out for commercial development.

JOCK: Huh?

NOVA: I wonder if it's zoned for subdivision.

JOCK: Nova, what the heck –

NOVA: That house would make one hell of a restaurant.

JOCK: Jesus, Nova. Why don't I buy you the White House so you can turn it into a Stuckey's?

NOVA: That place is bigger than the White House. Hell, it's big enough to turn into a theme park. A Gone With the Wind theme park. Gone With the Wind Theme Park! Can't you just picture it? Experience the magic of the greatest motion picture of all time. Dance the Virginia Reel with Rhett Butler. Flee the burning of Atlanta, help Scarlett deliver Melly's baby. Jock!

JOCK: What did I marry?

NOVA: I'd do anything to get that plantation away from Pougie. How am I gonna get him to sign it over to us instead of Fidel Castro? (*Pause.*) I could dress up like a sexy Cuban temptress and seduce Pougie –

JOCK: You can just give that idea a rest. No wife of mine is going to dress up like a foreigner and wiggle her how-de-do in that old gentleman's face.

NOVA: You're right, I could never pull it off. When it comes to show biz, I'm managerial, not actorial. Wait a minute. Remember that night you went on as Nina in the Seagull – back at the dinner theatre – that night Cheryl Swanson had her twins?

JOCK: That was an emergency.

NOVA: Your Nina was sexy, you had every guy in the audience fooled. And in prep school – you told me yourself – you played all the female leads – Saint Joan – Desdemona – Hell, you played Anita in West Side Story.

JOCK: It was a boy's school. There weren't any girls. Somebody had to do it.

NOVA: Well, somebody has to do it now, and it's going to be you. We're gonna dress you up like a Cuban bombshell, take you to that pig roast, tell Pougie you're on a mission from Castro, and get him to sign that plantation over to you. Then we'll have it. We'll have Arcadia.

JOCK: No way, Nova. That is out of the question.

NOVA: I'm not asking you a question. I'm telling you.

JOCK: (*Adamant.*) No way.

NOVA: (*Sniffing.*) Well then we've lost it. We've lost Arcadia. And Jock, that leaves me no alternative –

JOCK: Nova –

NOVA: – but to drag myself down to the Drunken Buzzard and beg them to give me a job as a topless waitress on the graveyard shift . . .

JOCK: You don't need to work. I'm a millionaire.

NOVA: I need my career! I need my self esteem! I need my theme park!

JOCK: Alright, Nova. I'll do anything it takes to make you happy. I'll dress up as a woman. I'll do whatever I have to to get you your theme park.

NOVA: Oh, Jock. (*They embrace.*) And if you're really good, I'll consider letting you play Scarlett at my Gone With the Wind Theme Park.

JOCK: Ha. I could too. (*A wave of sentiment.*) You know Nova, if one of us ever passes away, I hope I go first.

NOVA: Oh Jock. Me too. Now go get your costume together.

JOCK: Cuban bombshell . . . Cuban bombshell. (*Exiting, singing.*) "Tonight, tonight, won't be just any night." (*He exits.*)

NOVA: (*Tara's theme swells.*) "Katy Scarlett O'Hara, land is the only thing worth living for, worth fighting for, worth dying for . . . "

(*With a flourish, Nova clicks off the television set with the remote control, then exits, singing and sashaying.*)

"I want to be in Arcadia, nothing but me in Arcadia."

DOG LOGIC
by Thomas Strelich

Serio-Comic / 1 Man, 1 Woman
> Hertel: a man suffering from brain damage after being
> shot in the head by his father, 30-40
> Anita: his mother, a wealthy real estate player, 60

The Setting: an old pet cemetery in a remote area of California's Central Valley, the present

Anita abandoned her son and husband when Hertel was quite young and went out into the world to make her fortune. When Hertel's land becomes valuable to a powerful real estate concern, Anita returns, expecting to be able to make some money. As she is to discover, Hertel is determined to keep his home. Here, mother and son share their first conversation in 30 years.

O   O   O

ANITA: (*Calling toward the house.*) Where is he anyway?
HERTEL: (*Off.*) Who?
ANITA: Your dad.
HERTEL: (*Off.*) Out there. With the rest of 'em.
ANITA: (*Scanning the cemetery.*) Can you be more specific?
HERTEL: (*Off.*) See the pyramid thingy out there?
ANITA: Yeah.
HERTEL: (*Off.*) Dad's the first one to the left.
ANITA: Oh, ok. (*Pause, plays the accordion some more, stops.*) Is that . . .
HERTEL: (*Off.*) Yes, it's legal.
ANITA: (*Nods. Satisfied.*) He was a lot older than me, you knew that didn't you?
HERTEL: (*Off.*) Yeah. In round numbers.
ANITA: I was only seventeen. He was fifty, and some change. Told me he was thirty-nine. How the hell would I know the difference? Thirty-nine, forty-nine, fifty-nine, all the same to me – over twenty-one, that was my frame of reference.

Besides this was right after Bacall married Bogart so the whole thing had a certain . . . cachet. He ever tell you how we met?

HERTEL: (*Off.*) Nope. Just said you met in Bakersfield.

ANITA: Yeah, the Christmas parade. I was a majorette, the little white boots with the tassel in the front, hat, baton – the whole shot. Marched next to his Cadillac. He was the grand marshall you know. He just stared at me the whole parade. He waved at everybody like he was supposed to, but he never took his eyes off me. Of course, I was flattered as hell, a man of such stature in the community showing an interest.

HERTEL: (*Standing in the doorway, mopping, hoots and laughs.*) Stature? (*Goes back inside.*)

ANITA: I was from Boron, I was easily impressed – he had his teeth and he didn't blow his nose with his thumb. So anyway, he starts flying out to the desert all the time to see me, in his own personal airplane, a Beechcraft Bonanza, V-tail. Take me out flying, fly us over to Palmdale for dinner, things like that. Flew me over here to see this place once. It was beautiful out here back then, trees, grass, water – I was a desert rat, it was green, that was enough for me. Then for my eighteenth birthday, he flew us to Vegas and we got married. And then he sold the airplane. (*Pause.*) What's the pyramid for?

HERTEL: (*Off.*) Yappy.

ANITA: Oh. (*Pause.*) So anyway, and then I'm living here, in this place, with him, which is why I got this thing (*The accordion.*), for all the good it did. Turn around and I'm twenty-nine, living with a little boy and an old man, and I couldn't breathe anymore – asthma, from all the grass and trees – and nothing is like I thought it would be, and so I just left. My dad left us when I was little, so I guess it's a genetic thing. It was nothing personal. Nothing against you. (*Pause. Calling inside.*) How'd he die?

HERTEL: Heartworm. (*Entering with some cold drinks.*)

ANITA: Your father?

HERTEL: No, for hell's sake. Yappy.

ANITA: Oh. That's too bad. How'd your father die then?

HERTEL: Well . . . (*Thinks.*) . . . he died of a broken heart, Mom.

ANITA: Oh give me a break . . .

HERTEL: Took him, you know, like twenty years, but he did, he died of a broken heart.

ANITA: Bullshit.

HERTEL: I'm not saying there weren't complications – emphysema, kidney failure, liver disease, I mean these were certainly contributing factors. But primarily it was a circulatory problem . . . you. I waited outside the door, to your room, for the first few months, I guess thinking you'd show up somehow if I waited long enough. I mean the room was still full of you, you just weren't there to be seen, anymore. Pissed Dad off, (*Imitating.*) "She's dead, ya dumb sonovabitch, she's dead, she ain't coming back."

(*A lull. Anita looks at him tenderly, reaches out to put her hand on his shoulder. He moves away, unaware.*)

Every Christmas he'd get drunk, talk about you. Rest of the year you were dead of course. But when he got drunk at Christmas, you got . . . resurrected as it were.

ANITA: What'd he say?

HERTEL: The basics, how it was the happiest ten years of his life, stuff like that. About how if you'd been killed in a car crash or something, or like kidnapped from a parking lot by some serial killer and murdered and dumped in a ditch, about how he could have understood that, since that woulda been an act of God. But for you to just . . . leave like you did. It just seemed very . . . intentional to him, he could never understand that. All in all it made for a very unique holiday experience.

ANITA: (*Drawn from her thoughts.*) How would me being killed by some psycho be an act of God any more than me leaving on my own be an act of God?

HERTEL: Let's not bring God into the discussion, Mom, I'm just telling you what he thought, let's not muddy up the issue with religion here – I didn't know you were into that shit.

ANITA: Yeah well, kiddo, there's a lot of things about me you don't know.

HERTEL: I hear that.

ANITA: So happens I was, you know, born again. Right after I left here. This was before they even called 'em "born agains." Didn't use the generic term back then, just called 'em what they were, Four Square Baptist, Pentecostal – that's what I was, Pentecostal. Really got into it. Spoke in tongues, you know, roll my eyes back, faint, let other people catch me. I mean why do it at all if you're not going to go all the way? It really helped me. But, after a while, I kind of drifted away from Jesus, got into real estate.

HERTEL: (*Pause.*) Good career move. (*He putters around the garage, pointlessly moving junk from one pile to another.*)

DOWN THE SHORE
by Tom Donaghy

Serio-Comic / 1 Man, 1 Woman
   MJ: a young drifter, late 20s
   Luke: (really Lucy) his younger sister, 15

The Setting: the street next to a church outside of Philadelphia, the present

MJ has returned home after several years of drifting from job to job and is shocked that his little sister barely remembers him. Here, he asks her for a job in the family business.

○   ○   ○

MJ: Phoned you last week. Sal Sal picked up. Actually spoke to me. She told me you couldn't come to the phone cause you were packing for fat girl camp.

LUKE: Oh, my God.

MJ: What?

LUKE: Like *mention* fat girl camp.

MJ: Well –

LUKE: Not heffing.

MJ: Personally couldn't imagine you obese.

LUKE: Oh, my GOD!

MJ: She said you were getting to be the size of the tool shed.

LUKE: Not that fat!

MJ: Not at all!

LUKE: Mean, God, not porking!

MJ: . . . Know it. Mean, that's how I could take your bracelet.

LUKE: (*Pause.*) No way.

MJ: (*He takes a girl's bracelet out of his pocket.*) Slipped right off. Can still do it.

LUKE: But –

MJ: Can't do the ring trick anymore.

LUKE: You stole my bracelet.

MJ: Not STOLE –

LUKE: You cleptoed my –

MJ: It's magic.

LUKE: My bracelet –

MJ: Used to like it when you were a kid.

LUKE: Give it back.

(*He hands it to her.*)

You are some kind of a creepo, right? Stealing my –

MJ: Not steal.

LUKE: – bracelet, that is sick, that is schizoid.

MJ: Didn't steal.

LUKE: Oh, my God.

MJ: Gave it up.

LUKE: Yeah, can tell.

MJ: It's magic.

LUKE: Deeply troubled.

MJ: Used to like it.

LUKE: Nobody TAKES anything from me, (*To the statue.*) You believe this, Bern? Gone for decades he's got the inside dirt on my diet habits.

MJ: Why you talk to her?

LUKE: 'Cause I sympathize 'cause she weighs so much. (*She walks to the street.*) Oh my God, he is dismembered body parts.

MJ: Sal Sal told me she turned my bedroom into a video library. True?

LUKE: Possibly.

MJ: Funny to think your room is a video library, you know? Bet stacked with pirated copies of every MGM film ever created. You know, bet a whole Esther Williams section. If she took it out she could fit my bed back in. But she won't probably.

LUKE: Dunnuh.

MJ: She has this thing about the fact that the last time I was home I set her bedroom on fire.

LUKE: Well . . . oops.

MJ: Mean, I was a kid, you know. Didn't mean to set the entire room – only her nightstand part of it. But things have a way of being –

LUKE: Sure.

MJ: Shockingly combustible in an extravagant way, you know, so –

LUKE: She was pissed.

MJ: Well, yeah.

LUKE: Yeah, sure.

MJ: That's something she probably brought up once or twice. I'd understand if she did.

LUKE: She says you –

MJ: Says?

LUKE: Never brings you up.

MJ: (*Pause.*) Remember every part of that house. Part where she's got her artsy-crafts table. Where she made holiday wreaths. Wreaths with the gourds? The plastic acorns?

LUKE: Believe those things?

MJ: Dried squash.

LUKE: She puts one on the screen door. For like some ridiculous holiday only Tarzanian people heard of, something. Told her, "Yo! BACK door screen door, NOT going on the front door!" Told her. They are so horrifyingly queer.

MJ: Well, they're not –

LUKE: Total 'mo to infinity.

MJ: They're seasonal things. She's attempting some art in the autumn of her life.

LUKE: Totally queer. Miniature scarecrows and shit? C'mon.

MJ: Well, yeah, guess. Never brings me up?

LUKE: Don't know if we need anyone in the office right now.

MJ: Oh, sure.

LUKE: To hire.

MJ: That's ok.

LUKE: Don't hire myself. Mean, I run the place but that aspect of it isn't an aspect of my responsibility. But could stop in Monday, ask Tulley.

MJ: Or Flynn. Flynn was my year.

LUKE: Flynn, yeah, cause I might be still –

MJ: Down the shore.

LUKE: Should be still, yeah. Tell them you're my brother or something.

MJ: Thanks.

LUKE: Kinda cool to be related to someone. Someone normal. 'Cept for the fact you're a clepto.

DREAM OF THE RED SPIDER
by Ronald Ribman

Serio-Comic / 1 Man, 1 Woman
Uyttersprot: a rag picker turned political informant, 40-50
Violet: a fish plant worker turned spy

The Setting: a country suffering under a military dictatorship

The conniving Uyttersprot has drafted Violet, the beautiful young woman he desires, into going undercover in the life of a suspected enemy of the people. Here, the repulsive man bargains for her affections with a ruby.

O   O   O

UYTTERSPROT: Sit down, Violet. We'll have a little drink and then we'll have a little talk.

VIOLET: (*Reluctantly sitting.*) I don't have all day. I have to rehearse, and then I have to get my legs waxed.

UYTTERSPROT: I brought a little surprise for you if I can find it, but first . . .

(*Pulling out a half-filled bottle of champagne and two crumpled and obviously used paper cups from his inside coat pocket.*)

. . . champagne!

(*Wiping out the cups with his fingers, blowing out whatever trace of dirt might be in them. Disgust is written all over Violet's face at this loathsome toad and his loathsome actions.*)

It's incredible what is being thrown out in the garbage these days. This was taken from the garbage of an honest judge who would not be corrupted; he would not wink his eye at the drug trade. He thought he was above the law until he got a hundred years in prison for not developing a convenient twitch.

(*Downing his drink and smacking his lips with relish. Noticing she's not drinking.*)

What's the matter? It's too warm? Wrong year?

(*Lightly sticking the tip of one of his fingers into her cup, testing the temperature.*)

VIOLET: The cup is dirty.

UYTTERSPROT: So what? Everything's dirty.

VIOLET: Somebody else's mouth was on it.

UYTTERSPROT: Somebody else's mouth is always on everything. Drink up. Drink up!

(*As Violet sips her drink.*)

Such delicate sipping like a little honey bee mouth. Drink up! Before the red spiders get here and there is no more drinking.

(*Violet empties her cup and Uyttersprot pours out another round.*)

As one spider said to the other, "Time sure is fun when you're having flies."

(*Laughing at his own joke, downing his drink.*)

So? How's business with you-know-who whose name is never allowed to be mentioned?

VIOLET: It's boring.

UYTTERSPROT: I put you in a great house with one of the great saviors of our country, a man known up and down the continent for his brilliant intellect, and you find it boring?

VIOLET: He has little tags of skin on his neck and he combs his hair every which way so nobody will see how thin it is and he's as old as you are.

UYTTERSPROT: Thank you. Thank you very much. This is the gratitude I get taking you out of the fish packing plant and molding you into your new identity as Mata Hari.

VIOLET: Who asked you to? I was happy at the fish plant.

UYTTERSPROT: You were not happy at the fish plant! You tried to commit suicide at the fish plant! If I didn't fish you out of the harbor at Antofagasta with my cane, you would have gone under for the thirty-second time!

VIOLET: I was happy at the fish plant! I had good friends!

UYTTERSPROT: You had no friends!

VIOLET: I had plenty of clothes and sheets of my own to sleep on!

UYTTERSPROT: You had one dress and it was stained front and back from where the men spread-eagled you on the market floor! And if you found wrapping paper to sleep in at night you were lucky!

VIOLET: I had . . .

UYTTERSPROT: Nothing!

VIOLET: I had . . .

UYTTERSPROT: Nothing and nothing and nothing but unredeemable selfishness and ingratitude! That is the quintessential nature of your existence, the sum of what you are made of, and the rest is whim! In all this world there is no truer love that the love Violet feels for Violet! Everything and everyone else you were born to betray! And sooner or later you will understand this about yourself, and you will not be floating around the air this way!

(*Pause.*)

So? How's business?

VIOLET: I think he loves me.

UYTTERSPROT: Good. How do you know this?

VIOLET: He told me.

UYTTERSPROT: So when's the happy wedding day?

VIOLET: I don't know. When do you want it? Do you want it?

UYTTERSPROT: March 5th. Is that all right?

VIOLET: March 5th is all right.

UYTTERSPROT: July 19th, August 12th, December 1st. Is that all right too?

VIOLET: That's all right, too.

UYTTERSPROT: All of them?

VIOLET: Any of them! All of them! Whatever!

UYTTERSPROT: It doesn't make any difference to you?

VIOLET: Why should it, as long as it doesn't interfere with my career?

UYTTERSPROT: What career?

VIOLET: You know.

UYTTERSPROT: Oh, that career.

(*Losing his temper.*)

Listen to me. The only career you have is to betray him! To get me his wife's clothes! To get him out of that monastery of a house he lives in so I can destroy him! That is your career! Not marriage! Not anything else!

VIOLET: (*Jumping to her feet, yelling back with equal ferocity.*)

My career is to be a famous performing artist! To go all over the world – Barcelona, Madrid, Europe!

UYTTERSPROT: (*Rising to his feet, provoked by her as only she* *can provoke him.*)

You are not going anywhere till I tell you where you are going! You don't even know where Europe is!

VIOLET: Oh! Oh!

UYTTERSPROT: What?

VIOLET: I've got a run in my stocking! All this yelling. It's your fault.

UYTTERSPROT: I'll get you another pair. Sit down.

VIOLET: You said I was going to be a performing artist.

UYTTERSPROT: Sit down and calm yourself. I am not going to put up with these ridiculous tantrums of yours that are getting worse and worse for no reason. I don't like unpredictable behavior.

VIOLET: You said I was going all over the world! That was what you promised me!

UYTTERSPROT: Sit down! If you want what I have for you in my pocket, sit down!

VIOLET: (*Remembering his promise, her curiosity aroused again.*) What have you got for me?

(*Sitting down, calming down.*)

UYTTERSPROT: That's better.

(*Sitting down.*)

That's my sweetheart. That's my beauty.

(*Stroking her hands, arms.*)

Outside the world is full of bones going clack clack in the alley. Inside here between us is peace and calm like chocolate melting in the sun, ice cream melting in the sun, the waves on the beach falling and falling.

(*Stroking her eyelids, her temples, his voice growing increasingly hypnotic. Her eyes flutter shut.*)

You are feeling very calm now and you are not upset because you remember that what I told you was that through me you would leap into a new life, you would become whatever it was that was truly inside you.

VIOLET: I am a great performing artist.

UYTTERSPROT: No. That is only your whim. It comes from all the lessons that I give you so that you can learn the skills necessary to be my secret agent, my Mata Hari. Everything done so that you might lure him down to this place for his destruction.

VIOLET: (*Her eyes opening.*)

I am going to Barcelona, Madrid, and Europe.

UYTTERSPROT: You are not going anywhere, but where I tell you to go.

VIOLET: (*Rising up in her chair, becoming all excited again.*)
I am going to be famous! I am going to be a star! I . . .

UYTTERSPROT: (*Rising up as excited as she.*)
You are not going to be anything but a betrayer of confidences, a traitor to the heart, false to the core and treacherous as the kiss of Judas! This is what I saw in the mind of the fish girl from the fish plant with the fish scales under every fingernail, and this is what will be in the end! That is the reality! The rest is whim and fantasy!

VIOLET: I want what you got in your pocket for me! And it better not be one of your cheap gifts! I'm sick and tired of your cheap gifts!

UYTTERSPROT: How dare you say that to me?

VIOLET: Because it's true! Everything you get me is cheap or broken or pulled out of the garbage a few seconds before the garbage truck comes.

UYTTERSPROT: And the lessons? You think that is cheap? You think it costs nothing to take someone like you and give in to her every whim to be a professional entertainer? To give her singing lessons, and acting lessons, and walking, talking, dancing, which-is-the-fork-for-the-lobster lessons?

VIOLET: (*Starting to walk away.*)
You only give me the lessons so I can be attractive to him! You said so yourself! So I could lure him down here!

UYTTERSPROT: (*Grabbing her by the shoulders, turning her around.*)
No! No! All I had to do was buy you some clothes, clean the stink of fish from your hands and put you down in front of him at one of his everlastingly stupid intellectual dinner parties, and that would have been sufficient! But I didn't do that, because I am a foolish man who gives in to your whims to the point of losing his sanity! And there is no cheapness to it, either! No cheap dresses! No cheap shoes! No cheap underwear and stockings! But you are never grateful! Nothing that could ever be done for you receives gratitude! You are a woman utterly without gratitude!

VIOLET: (*Aimlessly drifting about the table.*)

Am I really going to like this surprise, or is it going to be one of those worn-out heirlooms rich people are always trying to get rid of when they get poor?

UYTTERSPROT: Why don't you stick your hand in my pocket and find out?

VIOLET: (*Circling Uyttersprot, as warily as coy.*)
Which pocket?

UYTTERSPROT: Enny, meanny, miney, moe.

VIOLET: You pick.
(*Sitting down in expectation. Uyttersprot sits down and reaching into one of his many pockets pulls out a packet wrapped in white tissue paper and tied with a violet ribbon. Violet is suspicious.*)
It's not in a box?

UYTTERSPROT: I wrapped it myself.

VIOLET: I knew it! I knew it! If it was worth anything it would come in a box from a store! A real box from a real store!

UYTTERSPROT: Not all the time!
(*Calming down, trying to keep control of himself in the face of intolerable exasperation. Holding it out to her.*)
Well, take it and open it up. I can see you're interested. Whenever you're really interested in something your eyes light up like a cheap garnet around a fat lady's throat.

VIOLET: Is it a jewel? Is that what it is?
(*Just looking at the extended gift in Uyttersprot's hand, almost like a child in her sense of anticipation. And then she suddenly grabs it, tearing at the wrapping paper.*)

UYTTERSPROT: You like it? It's a ruby from Cambodia.

VIOLET: Is it real?

UYTTERSPROT: Of course it's real!
(*Watching her turn the ring around and around in her fingers.*)
That's right. Turn it in your hand. See how it catches the light from the lamp? Red . . . red . . . deep as a pigeon's blood.

VIOLET: (*Lost in her contemplation of the stone.*)
Oh . . . so beautiful . . . so . . .
(*To Uyttersprot, as if it might suddenly be wrenched away.*)
It's mine? You're giving it to me?

UYTTERSPROT: Of course. It's yours.
(*Losing interest in Uyttersprot, going back to the ring.*)

UYTTERSPROT: It was on the finger of a Cambodian princess until the Khmer Rouge came and took away the finger and the ring. God knows how many princesses locked away in their seraglios have worn that ring, turned it in their hand the same as you are doing, catching it in the flame of stars and candles, thinking it would be theirs forever.

VIOLET: Is it mine forever?

UYTTERSPROT: Absolutely, Forever. Uyttersprot brings you a gift. Today champagne and rubies. Tomorrow, who knows? Maybe calamity and whirlwinds. Give me your hand, pretty Violet. The third finger of your left hand.

(*Takes her hand and slides the ring on it.*)

Oiled and cared for, who could tell the hand of a princess from the hand born to gut a fish?

THE GAMBLERS
by Val Smith

Serio-Comic / 3 Men, 1 Woman
>Jackson Hayes: a gambling reverend, 40s
>George Crossman: the gambler's capper, 20s
>Titus O'Bannon: a planter, strong and vicious, 50-60
>Eugenie O'Bannon: his wife, beautiful and eccentric, 20-30

The Setting: a sidewheeler making its return down the Mississippi from St. Louise to New Orleans, just prior to the Civil War

Mrs. O'Bannon wishes to escape from her tyrannical husband and has enlisted the aid of Crossman. Here, all parties share a meal in the elegant dining salon of the river boat.

O   O   O

HAYES: Merciful God, we thank thee for this bountiful meal. Grant that we may show the same measure of generosity and kindness to each other that, in your great wisdom, you have bestowed upon us here.
(All set to but are interrupted by.)
Lord, we are all sinners in your sight. We seek your understanding and ask your forgiveness for our transgressions, past and present –
(A pause and some confusion as to whether Hayes is finished.)
– Guide us in your will, O Lord. Amen.

ALL: Amen.

MRS. O'BANNON: Nicely spoken, Reverend. What church did you say you were with?

HAYES: The Ouachita Baptist Church, ma'am.

MRS. O'BANNON: I cannot say I've heard of it.

HAYES: I'd be surprised if you had. Just a small congregation. But what it lacks in numbers, it makes up for in spirit.

MRS. O'BANNON: Isn't that charming, Mr. O'Bannon? I always thought Baptists opposed alcoholic libation. Am I mistaken.

HAYES: No. *(He sips his wine.)*

MRS. O'BANNON: But your congregation does not follow that particular rule.

O'BANNON: The Reverend is a tolerant man.

MRS. O'BANNON: My point was we wouldn't wish to offend.

O'BANNON: No chance of that.

HAYES: I was telling Mr. O'Bannon earlier, my principle in the matter of human frailty is one of tolerance. A little alcohol now and again. In moderation, of course. Where's the harm?

MRS. O'BANNON: Very commendable, Mr. Hayes. Don't you think, Mr. Crossman?

CROSSMAN: Oh. Surely.

(*They eat in silence. Joseph has brought the champagne and poured it for Mrs. O'Bannon.*)

MRS. O'BANNON: To kindness, generosity – and tolerance.

(*She takes a deep drink from her glass.*)

O'BANNON: Mrs. O'Bannon!

MRS. O'BANNON: Mr. O'Bannon?

HAYES: Champagne drunk too quickly brings on the vapors.

MRS. O'BANNON: Oh. Then I shall be more careful. More moderate.

O'BANNON: Damn right.

MRS. O'BANNON: Titus!

CROSSMAN: Sure is hot.

HAYES: Should have seen him this afternoon. You was wet through.

MRS. O'BANNON: Do you have a fever Mr. Crossman? You look feverish. Don't you think so Mr. Hayes?

(*She pours herself another glass.*)

CROSSMAN: Your concern is appreciated, ma'am, but I'm quite well.

MRS. O'BANNON: Perhaps it's love.

O'BANNON: Perhaps is what "love?"

MRS. O'BANNON: Strong emotions, especially that of love, can result in fever.

CROSSMAN: I assure you I don't have a fever, ma'am.

HAYES: I don't know. Dallying with ladies can be a strenuous business. So I'm told.

CROSSMAN: I was taking a nap, Reverend.

O'BANNON: Don't marry any of 'em.

MRS. O'BANNON: Mr. O'Bannon must mean you to learn from

his example.

O'BANNON: That's not amusing, Mrs. O'Bannon.

MRS. O'BANNON: I was speaking in jest, Titus.

O'BANNON: I wouldn't marry a woman who dallied back. That's all I meant.

CROSSMAN: I was takin' a nap, sir.

MRS. O'BANNON: And yet you married me.

O'BANNON: I courted you. I didn't dally. And neither did you. There's the difference.

MRS. O'BANNON: Excuse me, Mr. O'Bannon, but in some minds, there might be little difference between courting and dallying. Or, if there is, dallying might well lead to courting.

O'BANNON: Dallying is not honorable.

MRS. O'BANNON: Shame on you then, Mr. Crossman.

CROSSMAN: I was taking a nap!

O'BANNON: I never said that.

MRS. O'BANNON: Your statement implied Mr. Crossman's dallying was dishonorable.

O'BANNON: The man was taking a nap!

CROSSMAN: I was. Really!

HAYES: You're being teased, George.

MRS. O'BANNON: But suppose if poor Mr. Crossman *had* been dallying –

O'BANNON: –Leave it alone woman. Stop talking rubbish and let the man eat his supper. Take my advice, boy. Stay clear of 'em.

MRS. O'BANNON: The ladies, he means, Mr. Crossman. My husband has a quaint sense of humor. So dry you'd hardly notice to laugh.

O'BANNON: Be quiet and eat your food.

CROSSMAN: It surely is hot this evenin'.

I HAD A JOB I LIKED. ONCE.
by Guy Vanderhaeghe

Dramatic / 1 Man, 1 Woman
Les: a lonely outsider accused of assaulting a girl, 18
Tracy: a self-centered girl driven to acts of cruelty by peer
pressure, 17

The Setting: a car, 1967

Les maintains the swimming pool at the local club. He longs to
be accepted by the kids whose parents are club members,
especially pretty and popular Tracy, who bums cigarettes from
him all summer long. When someone starts writing terrible
things about his mother on the bathroom walls, Les turns to
Tracy, hoping that she will reveal the identity of the author.
Here, Les finds out more than he bargained for.

○　　　○　　　○

(*Tracy enters wearing sandals, skirt and halter top. She pauses,
trying to make out the car and its driver, then approaches
hesitantly, not sure who it is calling to her.*)
LES: It's me, Trace!
(*Tracy pokes her head into the open door, finally recognizes
Les.*)
TRACY: Oh, it's you. I didn't know who it was at first.
LES: Yeah, well it's me. Can I give you a ride somewheres?
TRACT: (*Looking around the inside of the car.*)
I didn't know you had a car, Les. When did you buy this old
reservation beater? (*Ironically.*) Nice wheels.
LES: (*Embarrassed and stiff.*) It's the old man's.
TRACY: (*Laughing.*) Oops. Apologies to the head of the
household.
LES: (*Trying to make light of the situation.*) So can I give you a lift
anywheres in my junker?
TRACY: (*Looking back in the direction from where she came.*)
I don't think so, Les.
LES: (*Insistent.*) It looked to me like you were going somewhere in

a hurry. Really stepping out. Even this rust bucket's faster if you're in a hurry.

(*Les waits for an answer while Tracy, silent, gazes back over her shoulder.*)

So what do you say?

TRACY: (*Making up her mind.*) All right.

(*She hops in, settles herself on the seat.*)

LES: (*Touching the brim of an imaginary chauffeur's cap.*)

James at your service, ma'am. Where to?

TRACY: The Dog'N Suds. (*Sharply.*) No, not there. Oh, I don't know. Anywhere. Just drive.

LES: Done.

(*He drives the car away from the curb. He drives while Tracy sits stonily beside him. He casts quick glances her way, trying to gauge her mood.*)

If you smell anything funny – well don't think it's me, eh? The old man forgot his lunch – a sardine sandwich – in the glove compartment last weekend. Sardine seems to have killed the air freshener. (*Laughs nervously.*) I got one dead pine tree in this car, I guess.

(*Tracy smiles condescendingly.*)

You want the radio? I can get Winnipeg. The car's a piece of junk but the radio's pretty good. You want the radio on?

(*He reaches out to switch the radio on.*)

TRACY: (*In an expressionless but commanding voice.*) Leave it off.

LES: Sure. Sure thing, Tracy.

(*They drive on for a while, Les repeatedly rubbing his nose and darting furtive looks her way.*)

You thinking, Tracy? Because if you're thinking I don't want to interrupt. (*Lamely.*) If you're thinking.

TRACY: Bob and I just had a fight.

LES: (*Unable to disguise his delight.*) Who? You and Bob Marsh? Bob the Bog?

TRACY: We broke up. After only a month of going steady. I can't seem to make a go of anything with a guy.

LES: Well . . . with him maybe. But really, he's a grade A dork. Who could? I mean make a go of it. With him.

TRACY: (*Turning to Les.*) He makes me so mad sometimes! He's the most selfish, inconsiderate person – Tonight there's this party – probably the last party of the summer – and I asked him:

Could he please get me a bottle of crème de menthe for the party? I love crème de menthe. And so he forgets or something, he was out golfing with his father, some lame excuse, and he claims it was too late for him to find somebody to pull him a bottle before the Liquor Board closed. And so we had this big fight and I told him what I thought of him and now I guess I get to miss the party. (*Pause.*) So what do you think of that?

LES: (*Shakes his head.*) Pretty shitty.

TRACY: (*Settling back with her arms hugging her breasts.*)
So if I seem moody and unsociable, you know the reason why. (*Keeping silent they drive on for a time.*)

LES: (*Summoning up his courage.*) Tracy?

TRACY: What?

LES: I was thinking - maybe you don't have to miss the party. (*Hurrying on as if in fear of being stopped.*) I could go to the poolroom and pay somebody to pull us a case of beer from off-sale. I know it's not crème de menthe but it's booze, right? So if the two of us went to this party, like together, we'd have something to drink and it wouldn't be so bad and you might have a pretty decent time anyway.

TRACY: (*Appalled by this suggestion.*)
No . . . no, I don't think so, Les.

LES: (*Excited by his proposal.*) If you're afraid that Bob maybe'll kick up a fuss or something like that –

TRACY: It's not that, Les.

LES: (*Brought up short.*) What then?

TRACY: Well, the party's private kind of. Invitations only. So it would be . . . awkward.

LES: Like I would be about as popular as syphilis is what you're saying.

TRACY: I said awkward. Don't put words in my mouth.
(*Both stare straight ahead, tight-lipped, tense.*)

LES: What's wrong with me, Tracy?

TRACY: What are you talking about?

LES: (*Passionately.*) I'm talking about the pool, about the things that people write on the changeroom walls. Things they write about my mother, knowing it's me that has to clean them up.

TRACY: (*Staring out the side window.*) People get bored. They like to stir things up a bit.

LES: Who's doing it, Tracy? Who's writing that stuff?

TRACY: (*Still looking out the window.*) Search me.

LES: You're at the pool all day. You'd hear them laughing about it. Where's the joke if nobody knows who's doing it?
(*He waits for a reply. None comes.*)
I done you a lot of favors this summer, didn't I? Can't you do me this one? It's driving me crazy. In the morning, before I go into those washrooms my stomach is upset, like before a big test – only worse, a lot worse.

TRACY: Speaking of bored, Les. Change the record why don't you?
(*She turns away from the window to Les.*)
Read my lips. (*Slowly and carefully she enunciates.*) I . . . don't . . . know. (*Pause.*) Is it sinking in?

LES: If you'd just maybe even hint –

TRACY: (*Angrily interrupting.*) All right, that's it. Take me home. Here I'm having one of the worst nights of my life and you've suddenly got to start in on me with this crap which I've told you, I can't count how many times – at the pool even – that I don't know anything about and I don't care to know anything about, I'm not interested in who's writing on what walls what things and still you won't leave it alone.

LES: I don't mean to upset you, Tracy. But don't you see? This business keeps going around in my head, it doesn't let up on me, I think about it all the time –

TRACY: (*Holding up her hand, speaking coldly and peremptorily.*) Not another word, Les.
(*Les lapses into a restive silence.*)

TRACY: (*Conciliatory.*) If you can be good company, if you can be nice, Les, you don't have to take me home. Can you do that?
(*Les makes no reply.*)
All right then, take me home. There's one thing I can't stand, it's a sulker.

LES: I'm not sulking.

TRACY: You are. You're acting like a big cry baby, feeling sorry for yourself. And who's the one who broke up tonight?

LES: You.

TRACY: You got it, mister. Me. Tracy broke up with somebody tonight.

LES: Consider yourself lucky.

TRACY: Well! As a matter of fact, I don't feel lucky! Maybe I cared for Bob Marsh.

LES: Why? I mean what is it with the guys I seen you going out with ever since maybe grade eight?

TRACY: This is my street! You can drop me right here! Last house on the end. (*Pointing.*) That one right there, just stop the car.

LES: (*Stops the car. Turns off the keys. Squints through the windshield at the house.*)

I bet you got a fireplace in your house.

(*Turns to Tracy.*)

You got a fireplace in your house?

TRACY: (*Puzzled, bobs her head.*) Sure we have a fireplace.

LES: (*Looking at the house.*) I bet you got a rumpus room. You got a rumpus room in your house?

TRACY: Yes.

LES: I bet you Bob Marsh has a rumpus room and a fireplace in his house. Am I right?

(*Tracy nods.*)

And every boyfriend you've had since you were twelve years old – all those stupid horses' patoots I've seen you with – I bet every one of them had a rumpus room and a fireplace in their houses too.

TRACY: What if they did?

LES: And I bet they all have to have certain kinds of clothes, desert boots and like that. No pointy-toed black shoes. And tans. You never went out with a guy who didn't have a pretty nice tan, Trace? Didn't look like one of the Beach Boys?

TRACY: You tell me. You seem to be the expert. Why you acting like this all of a sudden?

LES: (*As if he doesn't hear her.*) I work at a swimming pool and here I am, white as Casper the Ghost. (*Beat.*) Ever seen me at the grill watching one of your pool parties, Trace? Not likely.

TRACY: Get normal, Les.

LES: That's my summer right there, Trace. Dead white. You ever seen skin so pale?

TRACY: Oh sure. Les'd *have* to be the whitest. Check me out, you want to see fair skin. In a mirror, naked, I look like I'm wearing a white bikini.

LES: (*To himself.*) It's not the same, Tracy. Big difference.

TRACY: Big difference! Look at that, big difference!

(*She turns down the front of her skirt, exposing her belly.*) There's white for you.

(*The way in which Les looks at her naked belly awakens Tracy to what she has impulsively done. She reaches out and takes hold of his arm, presses it down on her abdomen, ostensibly for purposes of comparison.*)

What'd I say? Every bit as white as you, aren't I?

(*Les does not say a word. He stares down dumbly at his arm lying where it does. Tracy assumes he is rendered speechless by the position he finds himself in.*)

What's the matter, Les? Cat got your tongue?

LES: (*Without lifting his head.*) Who's doing it Tracy? Who's writing that stuff about my mother on the changeroom walls?

TRACY: Excuse me, but I'm out of here. (*She prepares to leave the car. As she does, Les, head still hanging, tucks his hand into the waistband of her skirt and prevents her from going. Tracy, horrified, protests.*) Les! Les! What are you doing? Get your hand out of there, Les! (*Struggling.*) Let me go! Let me go or I'll scream!

LES: (*Hanging on grimly, head still bowed.*) So scream.

TRACY: (*Ceasing to fight, trying to imbue her voice with authority.*) I'm not telling you again, Les. I mean it.

LES: Not until you tell me.

TRACY: (*Throwing a fit.*)

You son of a bitch! Pervert! (*She claws and scratches his arm with a deliberate, furious intent to injure.*) Let me go!

(*Scarcely flinching, Les submits to the attack until Tracy realizes it is pointless. She falls back, panting, Les still doggedly hanging on.*)

LES: Finished?

TRACY: Creep. Loser.

LES: Who did it? Just tell me.

TRACY: You really want to know? All the guys. Don. Bob. They didn't go for a piss they didn't take a pen along.

LES: Why?

TRACY: Because you're so pathetic, that's why. Trying to wiggle and worm your way in where you don't belong. That's loser stuff, Les. Begging to be liked. It's pathetic. Grow a spine.

LES: (*Stunned.*) And the girl's washroom . . . ?

(*Tracy turns away, so as not to have to answer.*)
The girl's washroom?

TRACY: Who do you think?

(*Les is so shocked he releases his grip on her waistband. Tracy notes this.*)
You don't have any friends, so you don't understand how it is. They're my *friends*, Les. It was just a giggle.

LES: (*Shocked.*) Giggle?

TRACY: A game. My old man and my old lady counting the china. (*Pause.*) You and my mother, Les. Two peas in a pod.

LES: What?

TRACY: (*A confession.*) You're just like her. Maybe you and my mother think you're better than other people, but you're not. You're worse. Know why? Because you invite people to walk all over you like a door mat. Maybe Dad couldn't stop himself, even if he wanted to. (*Beat.*) It's sick. You think I don't want to like my own mother?

LES: That's nuts.

TRACY: (*Recovering her composure.*) Like my Dad says. There are two kinds of people in this world. People who get done to, people who do. My old lady gets done to. That's not for me!

LES: It's my mother we're talking about –

TRACY: Les, if you want to get even, go ahead, buy yourself a pen and write whatever you'd like about my mother. Do it!

LES: (*With an edge of hysteria.*) You can say that when it isn't true! It's different when it's true!

TRACY: If it's true, what are you complaining about? Anybody's entitled to say anything, as long as it's true. Ask my father, he's a lawyer.

LES: (*Growing more emotional.*) Don't you know anything about shame?

TRACY: Now you sound like my mother.

LES: Can't you guess what it feels like?

TRACY: I don't want to guess! (*Pause. Trying to distance herself from him.*) Really, Les. It's been a wonderful summer. Thanks for the loans, thanks for the cigarettes, most of all, thanks for the laughs. But I've got to be going.

LES: I'm here, Tracy! Goddamn it, I'm here! Look at me!

TRACY: (*Frightened.*) Les –

LES: You should know what it feels like.

TRACY: I'm going, Les.

LES: (*Seizing her waistband.*) Maybe I ought to send you home in your white bikini tonight. That'd get around, too. Tracy's white bikini. That's be as funny as any writing on a wall.

TRACY: Les!

LES: Tracy in her white bikini. (*Les gives a little tug to the waistband of her skirt.*) Oops and they're off.

TRACY: Les . . . don't act crazy.

LES: It's only fair, Trace. You said for me to get even. Let's do it! Let's get even.

TRACY: Les!

LES: Just so you know, Trace. Just so you know how it feels.

TRACY: (*Begging.*) Please, Les. I . . .

LES: They got to come off, Trace.

TRACY: No.

LES: Yes.

TRACY: Let go!

LES: I'm somebody, Tracy! I ain't this summer's joke! Maybe you are!

I KISSED ELVIS
by Jocelyn Beard

Comedic / 1 Man, 2 Women
Marva Rae Purdy: a woman obsessed with building a shrine
  to Elvis, 40-50
Portia Sue Danton: her Cajun housekeeper, 40-50
Lake Hugo: Marva Rae's nephew, a sleazy opportunist, 20-30

The Setting: a mansion on the Louisiana bayou, a few years
back

Lake has convinced Portia Sue to help him to gaslight Marva Rae
out of her millions. Their plan is to make this queen of all Elvis
fans believe that Elvis is returning to earth for her. Here, their
elaborate stratagem begins to unfold.

O   O   O

PORTIA SUE: (*Whispering.*) This here gi-tar is the eggzact model
favored by the King! Lake got it in one of them pawn shops
down to the Big Easy.
(*Portia Sue places the guitar beneath the mantle. She hears
Marva Rae approaching and quickly begins a flurry of cleaning
activity. Marva Rae enters with a copy of Satellite Week
magazine.*)
MARVA RAE: Portia Sue, will you kindly tell me how in hell to
figure out which satellite is playin; "Harum Scarum?" The
damn VCR is busted again and I . . .
(*Marva Rae sees the guitar and is struck dumb.*)
PORTIA SUE: Marva Rae, you know as well as I do that the only
person who can work that damn dish is Lake. Marva Rae?
Marva Rae? What's the matter with you, girl?
MARVA RAE: (*Pointing at the guitar.*) Where . . . where did that
come from?
PORTIA SUE: (*Casually, not looking up from cleaning.*) Where'd
what come from?
MARVA RAE: (*Whispering.*) That!
PORTIA SUE: What?

MARVA RAE: That! That! THAT!!!!

PORTIA SUE: Oh, you mean this old gi-tar? I 'spose it's Lake's. (*Marva Rae crosses to the guitar as if in a dream.*)

MARVA RAE: (*To herself.*) No . . . it couldn't be . . .

PORTIA SUE: I said: it must be Lake's.

MARVA RAE: (*Softly, shaking her head.*) No.
(*She reaches out and strokes the neck of the guitar.*)

PORTIA SUE: What's that, Marva Rae?

MARVA RAE: (*Tenderly picking up the guitar and cradling it.*) It's a miracle.

PORTIA SUE: (*Going back to her cleaning.*) It'll be a miracle if that boy stops leavin' his stuff all over the damn house.

MARVA RAE: You ninny, this isn't Lake's guitar!

PORTIA SUE: Well, whose is it?

MARVA RAE: His!!!

PORTIA SUE: Whose?

MARVA RAE: Portia Sue, this is a 1956 Gibson J-200. It's the guitar He always used. It's His.

PORTIA SUE: Don't be ridiculous, Marva Rae. It must be Lake's.

MARVA RAE: (*Clutching the guitar protectively.*) No!

PORTIA SUE: Merci Dio, what a fuss. (*Calling.*) Lake! Lake Hugo!

LAKE: (*Off.*) What's that, Portia Sue?

PORTIA SUE: Lake, get on in here.

LAKE: (*Off.*) Be right there!

MARVA RAE: It isn't Lake's, I tell you! It's His!!
(*Lake enters.*)

LAKE: What can I do for you ladies?

PORTIA SUE: Your aunt seems to think that your guitar, here is . . .

LAKE: (*Interrupting.*) Nice guitar, Aunt Marva Rae! Is this the latest addition to your collection?

MARVA RAE: (*Triumphantly.*) I told you!!

PORTIA SUE: Hold on, now, Lake. You mean to tell me this ain't your guitar?

LAKE: (*To Marva Rae.*) Wow, a Gibson J-200! Where did you find it?

MARVA RAE: I didn't find it, He left it here!

PORTIA SUE: Oh, for Heaven's . . .

LAKE: Who left it here, Aunt Marva Rae?

MARVA RAE: (*Reverently.*) He did.

LAKE: Who?

PORTIA SUE: (*Before Marva Rae can answer.*) Elvis! She thinks that Elvis crawled up out of his grave, found this old guitar and brought it here.

MARVA RAE: For the shrine.

LAKE: What's that you say, Aunt Marva Rae?

MARVA RAE: The shrine, Lake. He knows it's the One True Shrine.

PORTIA SUE: Now, Marva Rae; that's what you said about the black belt.

LAKE: What black belt?

MARVA RAE: Oh, Lake! You just wouldn't believe what's happened since you left for your business trip!

LAKE: (*Leading Marva Rae to a chair.*) You sit down, Aunt Marva Rae. You're getting yourself into a state. Now, tell me about the black belt.

PORTIA SUE: Lake, now don't you start caterin' to her delusions.

LAKE: Hush up, Portia Sue.

MARVA RAE: (*Whispering.*) Oh, thank you! She's been drivin' me to distraction with her skeptical nature. It's evil, I tell you. (*Loudly, to Portia Sue.*) Don't you have some cleanin' to do, Portia Sue Danton?

(*Portia Sue hrrmmphs and returns to cleaning.*)

LAKE: There, she can't hear us now, Aunt Marva Rae. Tell me about the black belt.

MARVA RAE: (*Checking to make sure Portia Sue isn't listening.*) Well, a few days after you left for New Orleans, I was sorting through my video tapes – to see which ones needed replacin' – when I heard a strange noise out on the balcony.

LAKE: What kind of noise?

MARVA RAE: Well, it was a kind of a thump.

LAKE: A thump?

MARVA RAE: Yes, as if someone had tossed something up onto the balcony. I had made up my mind to pay that noise no never mind, but then I heard . . . I heard . . .

LAKE: Heard what?

MARVA RAE: (*Whispering.*) The Voice.

LAKE: Whose voice? Portia Sue's?

MARVA RAE: No, no, no! THE Voice. HIS Voice. The Voice of the King.

LAKE: The voice of the . . . Oh! The voice of the king. My, my. Are you sure that's who it was?

MARVA RAE: Yes! Yes! I knew it in an instant! I could never mistake His Voice.

PORTIA SUE: Ha!

MARVA RAE: I will not be mocked in my very own domicile!

LAKE: Don't pay her any mind!

MARVA RAE: But . . .

LAKE: (*Prompting.*) You heard the voice?

MARVA RAE: (*Enraptured.*) Oh, yes! I'll never forget it as long as I do live!

LAKE: What did he say?

MARVA RAE: He said: Marva Rae, honey, go out on your balcony.

LAKE: Your balcony?

MARVA RAE: It was then that I remembered the thump. So I rushed right on out there!!

LAKE: And???

MARVA RAE: (*In hushed tones.*) I found this!
(*She pulls a karate black belt from her pocket and shows it to Lake.*)

LAKE: What's this?

MARVA RAE: It's His black belt.

PORTIA SUE: It's evidence of your *derangement.*

MARVA RAE: Oh, you evil unbeliever!

LAKE: But this don't look like a belt, Aunt Marva Rae. Where's the buckle?

MARVA RAE: It's His black belt, Lake! His Ka-ra-te black belt! Read what it says right there!

LAKE: (*Peering at the belt.*) Property of Kang Rhee Karate Institute. So?

MARVA RAE: (*Excitedly.*) In 1969 he signed up for classes at the Kang Rhee Karate Institute, 1911 Poplar Avenue, Memphis, Tennessee. He got lots of black belts. Lots!

PORTIA SUE: Well, that ain't one of them!

LAKE: Now just a minute, Portia Sue! Did you look at this here belt?

PORTIA SUE: I don't need to! She probably bought it on her last trip to Graceland, put it in her pocket and forgot about it.

MARVA RAE: You ignorant blasphemer! This is the most

precious . . .

PORTIA SUE: That scrap of cloth ain't worth a ferryman's franc!

LAKE: Ladies, please! Aunt Marva Rae, are you sure that you never saw this belt before that day on the balcony?

MARVA RAE: As sure as salt.

LAKE: And you never saw this guitar before?

MARVA RAE: (*Passionately.*) Never!

LAKE: (*Triumphantly.*) But, did you hear the voice today? Before finding the guitar?

MARVA RAE: Why . . . no.

LAKE: Then it couldn't be the same thing, could it?

MARVA RAE: (*Wailing.*) But where did this come from???

LAKE: Well, I suppose . . . (*Seeing something on the guitar.*) now just wait a minute, there's writin' of some kind on the back of that guitar - maybe it's the address of the real owner. (*Reading.*) . . . 3 . . . 7 . . .6 . . . 4

MARVA RAE: 3764! Did you say 3764?

PORTIA SUE: Uh-oh: deaf and dumb.

LAKE: Yep, 3764. That's all it says.

MARVA RAE: (*Hugging the guitar blissfully.*) It is a miracle!

LAKE: What is?

MARVA RAE: 3764 Elvis Presley Boulevard . . . .

PORTIA SUE: . . . Looneyville, USA.

MARVA RAE: No! Memphis! Memphis, Tennessee! 3764 is the street address of Graceland! Number 3764 Elvis Presley Boulevard! Oh, it is His! It is! Wait! Do you smell something?

PORTIA SUE: Only that gumbo that you used to call a brain.

MARVA RAE: (*Inhaling deeply.*) Oh, yes! Don't you smell that, Lake?

LAKE: (*Sniffing.*) Smell what, Aunt Marva Rae?

MARVA RAE: (*Ecstatically.*) Brut!

LAKE: Brute? Who's that?

MARVA RAE: Not Brute, Brut! Aftershave! It's His. I smell it as sure as I smell the bayou. It can only mean one thing!

LAKE: (*Bemused.*) I'm afraid you've lost me, Aunt Marva Rae.

MARVA RAE: He's here!

LAKE: Who?

MARVA RAE: HIM!

LAKE: (*Understanding.*) Oh! You're sayin' that Elvis is here?

MARVA RAE: Mmmm-mmmm, yes.

LAKE: Right now?

MARVA RAE: Oh, yes.

LAKE: Tell me, Aunt Marva Rae: do you see him?

MARVA RAE: (*Confused.*) See him?

LAKE: Is he, say, standin' by the mantle, or sittin' in that chair?

MARVA RAE: Well, of course not! He is no longer corporeal, as you very well know.

PORTIA SUE: Neither are your wits, it would seem.

LAKE: Well, then. If you're tellin' me that you can't see him because he no longer enjoys the pleasures of a physical body, then how is it you can smell him, Aunt Marva Rae?

MARVA RAE: (*In a hushed and reverent tone.*) Stigmata.

PORTIA SUE: *Merci Dio*!

LAKE: Come again?

MARVA RAE: Stigmata!

LAKE: Hold on now. Are you ascribin' elements of the divine to this olfactory experience of yours?

MARVA RAE: Well, naturally! All that occurs within the sacred confines of the One True Shrine possesses elements of the divine!

LAKE: I find this all fascinatin', Aunt Marva Rae, but I'll bet you a jug o' shine that one of the Boulier boys left this guitar here the day that they came to clean out the gutters, and that 3764 is just a coincidence.

MARVA RAE: But what about the Brut?

LAKE: A smell don't mean a ghost's been here, Aunt Marva Rae!

MARVA RAE: (*Stiffly.*) I had somehow expected more of you, Lake Hugo.

(*She rises and surveys Lake and Portia Sue.*)

I pity you. I pity you both. For your skeptical natures won't let Him into your hearts.

(*Marva Rae exits with the guitar.*)

JOHANNESBURG
by James Harrison

Dramatic / 1 Man, 1 Woman
   Joseph: a Dutch-Canadian farmer, 40s
   Johanna: his daughter, 17

The Setting: a farm outside a small town in Ontario, 1939

Joseph is a fundementalist Christian attempting to start his own church in a rural Ontario setting. To financially support his efforts, and fulfil his vision from God, he is willing to kill unwitting migrant negro farm workers after they have worked full summers in planting and harvesting his crops. This is the second year he has used his daughter, Johanna, to help him in the killing. She confronts him with her doubts.

O   O   O

JOSEPH: We should be clear on what we have to do.

JOHANNA: You're making him dig that pit to tire him out.

JOSEPH: He's strong. We need to make him tired.
   (Johanna goes to the sewing box. She fusses with it. Joseph watches her. She waits a long moment before speaking.)

JOHANNA: Why have we not talked about this? . . . He has a family.

JOSEPH: God will take care of his family.

JOHANNA: This isn't about God, is it? It's about money.

JOSEPH: We've been given work to do, to build a church and bring God's children to Christ. And yes, you're right, we need money to do that. But there will come a time, it will be soon, the signs are becoming clear, when God will demand that we account for ourselves. We will be lifted up to his glory. What are you afraid of, leifert?

JOHANNA: I keep praying that this time something will stop it.

JOSEPH: I see. Like the angel stopped Abraham. It's confusing, I know. These times, when our fear is the greatest, these are the times of God's greatest test. Think of what Job suffered, think of Abraham. He was the leader of God's chosen people.

God tested him. He had the courage.

JOHANNA: What would you do if God told you to sacrifice me, like he told Abraham to sacrifice Isaac?

JOSEPH: It's not the same. When God speaks to us –

JOHANNA: What would you do?

JOSEPH: Johanna –

JOHANNA: Answer me! Would you sacrifice me?

(*Pause.*)

JOSEPH: Yes, I would. If God called a man of faith . . . what choice would he have?

JOHANNA: No.

JOSEPH: If we don't answer what we know in our heart to be true, then . . . then what do we have left?

JOHANNA: We are going to kill him. Does that not mean anything to you?

JOSEPH: He isn't like us, Johanna. None of us stands alone in God's plan. We've been given a great responsibility. "And God blessed them. And God said unto them, have dominion over the fish of the sea, and over the fowl of the air, and over every living thing that moveth on the earth." In times like this, we must look to the courage of Job, of Abraham.

JOHANNA: What was Isaac thinking?

JOSEPH: What . . . I don't know what you mean.

JOHANNA: You always talk about Abraham. Abraham's suffering. Abraham's courage. What did Isaac think? His father tied him up. He laid on the wood. He raised a knife over Isaac's head to kill him. What did Isaac think? Did he think he had done something terribly wrong that his father would do this to him? . . . Did he fight? . . . Did he try to run away? . . . Or did he ask his father to forgive him?

JOSEPH: Are you asking me?

JOHANNA: Will you forgive me?

JOSEPH: Will you deny God? What He's asking us to do?

(*A long moment of silence.*)

JOHANNA: No.

(*Joseph watches her for a long moment before speaking.*)

JOSEPH: We'll do it the same way as last year. When he's done his work he will wash his face and hands at the pump. It's his way, and then he goes to the loft to sleep.

JOHANNA: What if Walker comes back?

JOSEPH: He won't. Mr Monroe will offer him a drink. They'll talk for at least an hour.

JOHANNA: He'll ask questions.

JOSEPH: No.

JOHANNA: They were friends.

JOSEPH: They were travelling together. Walker has no loyalty to anyone but himself. They would have left here and never seen each other again. Now. Are you all right?

JOHANNA: I . . . I have to start the supper.

(*She goes to the counter and shifts the pie fixings around to create room. Joseph watches her for a long moment, uncertain what to do.*)

JOSEPH: I'm going out to the field . . . to see how they're getting on.

JULIUS AND PORTIA JONES
by Brian Christopher Williams

O   O   O

Dramatic / 1 Man, 1 Woman
John: a coal miner dying of Black Lung, 50-60
Portia: his estranged daughter, 30s

The Setting: a home in a nearly deserted coal mining town in the Allegheny Mountains, the present

Portia escaped her abusive father and fled to California, leaving her infant son, Julius, behind. Here, she finally confronts the man who made her life a living hell.

O   O   O

PORTIA: Hello, Pa. (*Pause.*) The house hasn't changed. It's gotten older maybe, but then who hasn't? (*Nervous titter.*) I don't mean you, Pa. You look . . . How are . . . (*Sighs.*) It's been a long time. (*Pause.*) You're not going to make this easy, are you?

JOHN: What do you want?

PORTIA: Well, that's it, isn't it? no dillydallying. Cut straight to the . . . I'm here about Julius, Pa. Well, that's not why I came, but now that I'm here . . . I want to take him with me. I want to take him to Los Angeles. (*Pause.*) He's gifted. I think it would be good for him.

JOHN: You think it would be good for him, huh?

PORTIA: Yes, I do.

JOHN: Do you know how old he is?

PORTIA: He's fifteen.

JOHN: Yes, he is. He's fifteen years old.

PORTIA: Pa, I –

JOHN: – How old was you when you runned off?

PORTIA: Julius' age. Pa, don't do this.

JOHN: (*Bellowing.*) This is my house. You got no right to tell me what I can't do in my own house. (*Coughing fit.*) What made you think I wouldn't throw you out in the cold? What made you think I wouldn't go upstairs and get my .22 and shoot –

(*Portia breaks in with her dialogue.*) – you right between the eyes?

PORTIA: This isn't about me. This is about Julius.

JOHN: You don't know nothing about him.

PORTIA: I know that he has a chance. If there is some way he can get out of this stick burg, he has a chance.

JOHN: A chance of what?

PORTIA: A chance to be a musician. A chance not to be hungry. A chance at a better life.

JOHN: That's always been your problem. Always thinking you was better than everybody else.

PORTIA: A chance not to end up like you.

(*John makes a sudden move with his arm that makes Portia flinch, but he stops short of actually striking.*)

JOHN: You got some money now. You got some fancy clothes. You think that's enough. You think your fancy perfume's going to cover up the stench.

PORTIA: I don't know what you're talking –

JOHN: –The stench of a two-bit whore. Sure, you can look down on me. What am I? Just some know-nothing old coal miner. What about them 15 years, Clementine? What about them years after you runned off? Do your Hollywood friends know how you earned your money then?

PORTIA: Shut up.

JOHN: When they find out what kind of woman you are, how many of your Hollywood friends are going to shed a tear for you?

PORTIA: I do not have to explain my life to you. You of all people. I never intentionally hurt anybody. I never –

JOHN: – Tell that to your mother. You never hurt no one? Tell it to her. It killed her to see what you became.

PORTIA: You have no right.

JOHN: Didn't even come to your own mother's funeral.

PORTIA: This has nothing to do with Ma. This has nothing to do with you or me. This is about Julius. I only want what's best for him.

JOHN: What do you care after all these years? What do you care, Clementine?

PORTIA: For Christ's sake, he's my son.

JOHN: He's not your son.

PORTIA: Of course he is.

JOHN: You gave him up when you left here 15 years ago. You gave him up when you abandoned him. After the sacrifices your Ma made for you, adopting him like he was her own boy to keep you out of trouble. For what? The whole town knowed you was a slut.

PORTIA: Go to hell.

JOHN: Couldn't keep your legs closed. No better than them tramps that used to wait at the edge of the mineshaft on payday.

PORTIA: It should have been you that got buried instead of Barlow's father.

LIGHT SENSITIVE
by Jom Geoghan

Serio-Comic / 1 Man, 1 Woman
> Tom: a man turned into a recluse by his blindness, 30s
> Edna: a woman who has volunteered to read to Tom, 30s

The Setting: an apartment in Hell's Kitchen, the present

Tom has stubbornly refused any help from his friends following the accident that left him blind. Here, the equally stubborn Edna arrives at his apartment and refuses to leave until she does her job.

○   ○   ○

TOM: You're here like ten seconds you're already banging around the place like a maniac. I'll have a heart attack or something. Listen, Ida.

EDNA: Edna.

TOM: My friend Lou was wadda ya callit . . . he acted what you might call prematurely.

EDNA: Prematurely?

TOM: You see, he thought I was in need of someone to help out because he's feeling kind of guilty he's taking off with some chick, but uh, the fact is, Edna. I really don't need any help. I'm doing fine. I've got lots of people who drop by. Too many, in fact. I've got a whole network of people.

EDNA: What are you saying?

TOM: I'm saying I really don't need any help. So thank you and adios.

EDNA: You want me to leave?

TOM: No! "Adios" is Spanish for "have some milk and cookies!" Yes, I want you to leave.

EDNA: But I moved things aside for this today. I made other arrangements.

TOM: So read to one of your other people.

EDNA: I don't have any other people. You're my only client.

TOM: Ho boy . . .

EDNA: You're also my first.

TOM: Ug!

EDNA: On the way over here my father said reading for the blind was the stupidest idea I've ever had.

TOM: Bright man.

EDNA: He's never been right about anything. I'll be damned if he's right about *this*! You don't have a network.

TOM: She's serious.

EDNA: If you had a network, I don't think this place would look like this.

TOM: Look, lady. I don't give a crap what you think. There's been a mistake. You should never of come in the first place, understand? It's nothing personal. I just don't need any help. Okay? Thank you. Goodbye.

EDNA: No.

TOM: What?

EDNA: I said no. I'm not leaving.

TOM: You're not what?!

EDNA: I put aside these four hours and I'm going to spend them here. I don't care if we just sit here. I'll do it. I will.

TOM: Holy shit . . .

EDNA: I don't care if you feel so bad for yourself that you just want to rot away. I'll stand here and watch you rot. At least you won't rot alone. I'm not going. For all I care we can both stay here in stone silence listening to the sound of your insides getting hard and crusty.

TOM: You're not going to go?

EDNA: That's right.

TOM: I've asked you to leave but you're not going to.

EDNA: Correct.

TOM: (*Flabbergasted.*) This is . . . it's . . . I can't believe you would . . . Hey! All right, all right. Enough, sister. Scram. Get your ass out of here!

EDNA: I'm not leaving.

TOM: Hey, enough! Get out!

EDNA: No.

TOM: Get out!

EDNA: I said no.

TOM: (*Screaming.*) GET OUT!!! How could you . . . I said GET OUT!!! GET . . . OUT!!!

(*No reply.*)

I could toss you out of here. I hope you know that, lady. I could eject you *physically*.

EDNA: Perhaps.

TOM: No "perhaps" about it! I've lived twenty years in this apartment. I know every square inch. I'd have you in a corner in no time and out the door five seconds after that.

EDNA: Like I said . . . perhaps.

TOM: Please just go and the whole thing'll be forgotten.

EDNA: Uh-uh.

TOM: Hey, c'mon. I want you out of here.

EDNA: No.

TOM: Get out.

EDNA: No.

TOM: Get out!

EDNA: No!

TOM: Get out, Goddamn it!!! I said get out!!!

(*No reply.*)

Do a thing like this to me? My own home?!

(*Tom begins to slowly circle the table as Edna keeps her distance.*)

This is my home, understand? I want someone out – they're out.

EDNA: Go ahead. Just try and catch me.

TOM: You're out of here . . .

EDNA: Not so. I'm like a jungle cat. I can move like you wouldn't believe. I'll just skip and twirl my way around this room. Zip! Twirl!

(*Tom makes a sudden grab for Edna and stumbles. His hand comes to rest upon a broom. He breaks off the bristle end of the broom with astonishing ease, then brandishes the stick.*)

TOM: Okay, fine . . . Let's see you zip your way around this.

EDNA: What are you doing?

TOM: Real smart ass, aren't you?

(*Mocking her.*)

"I'm not going." We'll see about that.

EDNA: You're not going to hit me with that, are you?

TOM: It's up to you, babe.

EDNA: You wouldn't.

TOM: A man has the right to choose who stays in his own home.

EDNA: Put that down.

TOM: No.

EDNA: Put that down!!!

TOM: (*Mocking her.*) No!!!

EDNA: You swing that thing at me . . .

TOM: Uh-huh.

EDNA: You just swing that thing at me . . .

TOM: Oh, I'm going to swing it at you all right . . .

EDNA: You do and I'll . . . I'll . . .

TOM: You'll what?

EDNA: I'll . . .

(*Thinks – then.*)

I'll shoot you.

TOM: What!

EDNA: I'll shoot you. I've got a gun. And, believe me, I know how to use it.

(*Edna opens her purse, then snaps it shut.*)

There, it's out. If you do anything that looks like an act of violence against me – so help me God – I'll drop you like a rock.

TOM: A gun . . .

EDNA: That's right. I don't want to use it but if I have to I will.

TOM: What kind of gun is this, if I might ask?

EDNA: A silver one.

TOM: A silver one. Sounds dangerous.

EDNA: It does the job.

TOM: You carry a gun?

EDNA: This is New York. Doesn't everyone?

TOM: You don't have no gun.

EDNA: Think so?

TOM: Yeah.

EDNA: Pretty sure of yourself, aren't you.

TOM: East side lady from the Lamphouse don't carry no gun.

EDNA: Not even one who was mugged? . . . and told herself "never" again. No one does that to me again . . . *ever!*"

TOM: You're lyin'.

EDNA: You're positive?

TOM: Total bull.

EDNA: Then go ahead. Take a swing.

(*Edna crosses nearer to Tom and stands before him.*)

If you're so sure about your ability to know a complete stranger you can't even see . . . then knock my block off. Go on.

(*Edna silently picks up an empty beer bottle and holds the top end against Tom's forehead.*)

I'll put a bullet right in your thick head. Maybe it'll knock some sense into you.

(*Tom and Edna stay like this for the longest time as Tom tries to figure out if Edna is bluffing or not. He finally lowers his broom handle.*)

TOM: I need a drink.

(*He pours from his scotch bottle but it's empty.*)

EDNA: It's empty.

TOM: I can tell that!!!

(*Tom crosses to a cupboard and takes out a gift-wrapped bottle of scotch. He unwraps it quickly and pours himself some.*)

EDNA: Gift wrapped. Someone give you scotch for Christmas?

TOM: No, I was going to give it to Lou, but . . .

(*Catches himself.*)

What am I doing talking to you?! I don't want you here – you're not here!

EDNA: Lord, you're thick . . .

TOM: *I'm* thick. you're waving a loaded gun around and *I'm* thick. Look, lady. Here it is plain and simple. As of this very moment, you are not even here.

EDNA: I see.

TOM: I tried to deal with you rationally, but it didn't work. So you want to stay – stay. But you're not here. I'm going to go about my business like I always do. As if you're not even in this room.

EDNA: Do as you wish.

TOM: I will. You've got the dullest four hours of your life coming up.

EDNA: You've obviously never been to the opera.

TOM: Huh?

EDNA: Nothing.

LION IN THE STREETS
by Judith Thompson

O   O   O

Dramatic / 2 Men, 3 Women
    Sue: a woman realizing the end of her marriage, 30-40
    Lily: a woman having an affair with Sue's husband, 20-30
    Laura: Sue's friend, 30s
    Bill: Sue's husband, 30-40
    George: Laura's husband, 30s

The Setting: a dinner party, the present

When Sue and Bill's young son has a frightening premonition of death, Sue frantically seeks out Bill at a dinner party at a friend's house. There she discovers that Bill intends to leave her for Lily and that their marriage is a sham.

O   O   O

LAURA: There was nothing to do! Nothing bloody to do but sing in the church choir! And go to baked-bean suppers! The snow at one point was actually up to the second floor window.

BILL: No, she had the *gall* to ask my male students to, "Please leave the room," for her senior seminar. She did "not wish to be dominated by men." Where did that leave me, I asked her?

LILY: No, no, no, you have to pat the dough, pat it for ohh a good five minutes and then put it in the microwave for one, then take it out, then pat it again.

GEORGE: St. Paul said, "We are as vapour," what is it? Like "vapour vanisheth" or - something. "We are no more." So I got up this notion of Martians – being these – wisps of vapour . . . No, you see your problem is you want the aliens to be like you, you are anthropomorphizing, you . . .

LAURA: That's so boring. That's so knee-jerk boring.

BILL: And she launched into the most savage tirade –
    (*Sue rushes in, dressed in her sweatsuit and sneakers. Everyone turns and freezes, except Bill, who continues to talk until Sue's third "Bill."*)

SUE: Bill . . . Bill . . . Bill!!! We have to talk!

BILL: Sue! Hi! Who's with the boys?

SUE: Mum came over. Bill, I need to talk, NOW.

LAURA: Would you like a drink, Sue? We have . . .

GEORGE: Yeah, come in and sit down.

SUE: No, no thank you. I just . . . want to talk to my husband.

BILL: Oh – okay, Sue, I'll just finish this conversation. Anyway -

SUE: He thinks he's going to die.

BILL: Who?

SUE: Timmy! Your son! He –

BILL: What, did he say that tonight? Oh, that's just kids, he's –

SUE: BILL, come home, your son is depressed his father is never there, why are you never never . . .

BILL: Sue PLEASE, we'll talk about it later, okay? So as I was saying, Laura . . .

SUE: Come with me.

BILL: I'll come in a while. I'll just finish this conversation, and then I'll come, okay

SUE: YOU COME WITH ME NOW!

BILL: Sue.

SUE: Bill, I need you, please, why won't you come?

BILL: Why won't I come? Why won't I come? Because . . .
(*Bill walks over to the others.*)
I'm . . . not . . . I am not coming home tonight.

SUE: Bill! Stop it, this is private –

BILL: It is not private, Sue, nothing we do is private for Christ's sake, you tell your friends everything, they all – know – everything – about us, don't they? How many times we had sex in the last month.

LAURA: I don't think that's true, Bill.

GEORGE: I haven't heard anything.

SUE: Bill, I think you're being very unreasonable. (*There is an awkward pause in which Bill and Sue lock eyes.*)

LAURA: (*To Lily and George.*) Well, it's a lovely night out there. Why don't the three of us go for a walk?

BILL: No.

SUE: You stay and finish up that wonderful looking chocolate paté, Laura, I'm sure you spent a lot of time on it. I'll just get Bill's coat and we'll go on home.

BILL: There is . . . somebody else, Sue. And I will be going home with her.

GEORGE: I think we've all had a little too much to drink, why don't we just . . .

SUE: Don't worry, guys, this isn't real. He's just drunk, he's just trying to scare me because we had this argument about the new sofa – Come on honey, let's go home. Who is it. Who is it, Bill? She's not here, is she? You didn't, you didn't bring her to my neighbors', OUR friends' dinner party, to which I was invited. Laura! Laura for God's sake.

LILY: It's me.

(*Sue laughs.*)

Why do you think I'm joking?

SUE: (*Looks at Lily, looks at Bill.*) Bill?

BILL: This is – Lily.

LILY: How do you do, Susan?

SUE: Don't you call me by my name you FAT!! Please, I don't think you know what you're doing. This is not just me, this is a family, a family, we have two children.

LILY: I'm sorry.

SUE: Bill you are not leaving your children.

BILL: Sue, please.

SUE: YOU TOOK A VOW! In a CHURCH in front of a priest and my mother and your mother and your father and you swore to LOVE and honor and cherish till DEATH US DO PART till DEATH US DO PART, BILL, it's your WORD your WORD.

BILL: I am breaking my word.

SUE: No.

BILL: YOU turned your back on me! You you – look at you in that . . . sweatsuit thing you're not – I mean look at her, really, you're you're you're a kind of . . . cartoon now, a . . . cartoon mum a . . . with your day-care meetings and neighborhood fairs, you know what I mean Laura. Your face is a drawing, your body, lines. The only time, the only time you are alive, electric again is . . . when you talk on the phone, to the other mums, there's a flush in your face, excitement, something rushes through your body, you laugh, loudly, you make all those wonderful female noises, you cry, your voice, like . . . music, or in the park, with Timmy and John, while they cavort with the other children at the drinking fountain, spraying the water and you talking and talking with all the mothers, storming, storming together your words like crazy swallows, swooping and pivots and . . . landing . . . softly on a branch, a husband, one of us husbands walk in and it's like walking into . . . a large group of . . .

LILY: You see, I love . . . his body, Sue. I mean, I really love it. I love to suck it. I love to kiss it, his body is my God, okay? His body –

(*Sue slaps Lily twice.*)

SUE: YOU . . . DON'T LIVE ON THIS STREET. You don't belong in this neighborhood.

(*Lily contains herself from slapping Sue back.*)

Where did you meet this . . . woman? On the street?

(*Bill starts to try to answer.*)

In a house of prostitution? I demand to know –

LILY: I fucked him on the telephone, Susan, many many times.

SUE: That is a disgusting . . . lie.

LILY: Come on Suzy, don't you remember? You caught him a couple of times, on the downstairs phone with his pyjamas around his ankles, he told me!

SUE: (*The wind totally out of her.*) I thought he was making . . . obscene phone calls.

BILL: Hello.

LILY: Hi there.

BILL: You got back to me quickly.

LILY: Fucking right.

BILL: Fucking right.

LILY: Your voice makes me crazy.

BILL: My voice.

LILY: I'm wet, Bill, wet just from hearing your voice.

BILL: What are you wearing?

LILY: Black silk underwear, red spiked heels, black lace bra.

BILL: Yeah? And what do you want? What do you want?

LILY: I want to suck your big cock, Bill, would you like me to do that? Would you like me to suck your big cock?

BILL: Oh baby, baby.

LILY: And then I want you to fuck me from behind all night long, can you do that? Can you do that for me, Bill?

BILL: Yes, yes, oh yes! Yes! Yes!

LILY: Oh, Bill!

SUE: BILLLLLLLLLLLLLLLLLLLLLL!!!!!!

(*She physically attacks Lily.*)

Aghhhh! Listen you, if you take my husband away from me and my children I will . . . kill you, I will, I will . . . come when you are sleeping and I will pull your filthy tongue out of your filthy mouth. And then I will . . . feed it to our cat.

BILL: Susan.

SUE: (*Forced laugh.*) I didn't mean that, I really didn't. I'm sorry everybody. This is all just so ridiculous and embarrassing and I'm sure we'll all laugh about it someday. I KNOW we will, but um . . . Bill? Won't you just . . . give me a chance? To show you? That I can? Be sexy? Cause I can, you know, much much more so than THAT creepy shit . . . Don't you remember? Don't you remember before we were married how you loved to watch me dance? Come on, you did? Remember, remember that wedding, Kevin and Leslie's? I wore that peach silk that you loved so much, that dress drove you crazy! And after the wedding we were in that room in the Ramada Inn over the water and I danced? You lay on the bed and you just . . . watched me, you loved it. I . . . whooshed whooshed in that dress, back and forth to this thing on radio back and oooh and back and you were laughing and and (*Laughs.*) and whoosh.

(*Music beats louder, filling the room, and Sue begins a slow strip tease.*)

And whoosh . . . and . . . close to you, you're hard . . . and far away and . . . turn . . . and whoosh . . . and . . . let . . . my . . . hair . . . down . . . you – love my hair whoosh and . . . zipppper . . . whoooo down so slowwwwwww turn and turn. . . you watching lying on the bed and ease . . . off my shoulders, you love my shoulders, elegant, ohh Billy, and down. Over my body the soft silky down and whoooooooooooooooooo whooOOOOOOOO Billy. Take me home Billy, take me home and let's make mad passionate love! Please.

(*Bill and Lily leave. George and Laura pick up Sue's clothing and bring it to her. Laura dresses her.*)

LAURA: Honey, I'm sorry.

SUE: Aghh, don't feel sorry for me, it's fine, everything will be fine because . . . his colon cancer's gonna come back, don't you think? Dr. Neville said he had a sixty-forty chance, it will. And she'll drop him, for sure, don't you think? And he will let me nurse him, I will . . . feed him broth, with a spoon, like I did my mum, and I will hold, I will hold his sweet head in my chest till, till his lips are black and his eyes . . . like bright dead stars ad he is dead and I will stay, I will stay with his body, in the hospital room because I did love that body . . . oh I did *love – that – body* once.

LOOSE KNIT
by Theresa Rebeck

Serio-Comic / 1 Man, 1 Woman
  Bob & Liz: a couple having an affair, 30s

The Setting: an apartment in Manhattan, the present

Bob has been sleeping with his sister-in-law, Liz, who here tells him that she doesn't want to see him any more.

○   ○   ○

LIZ: Bob, come on, this is crazy, she's going to be here any second.
(*He pulls her back and kisses her again. They end up on the table. This kiss begins to get passionate. Bob is clearly trying to take off Liz's clothes. She starts to take off his clothes, then stops herself.*)
Oh, God, what are we doing? What am I – oh, man –

BOB: Don't think. Liz. Just don't think.
(*He reaches for her. She pushes him away.*)

LIZ: Bob, this is clinical. I mean, do we want to get caught, much? What are you doing here?

BOB: I'm picking up the car. She's driving here and I'm supposed to drive away.

LIZ: See, this is my point.

BOB: Come on, Lizzie. Let's just tell her.

LIZ: Oh, that's a great idea. I'm looking forward to that. While we're at it, let's tell my parents, too. And your daughter.

BOB: I want to marry you.

LIZ: Yeah, well, I want world peace.

BOB: Come on . . .

LIZ: Bob, I am not going to marry you! You're already married! To my sister. God help me; you're married to my sister. I'm going to hell.

BOB: We can do this, Lizzie.

LIZ: Look, I don't want to talk about this now. It's giving me a headache. Oh, fuck me. This is the worst idea I've ever had.

It's hostile. Let's face it, this whole situation is very hostile.

BOB: I thought you loved me.

LIZ: Oh, please don't do this to me.

BOB: Do you love me or not?

(*She does not answer for a moment, then turns away.*)

LIZ: I have to get ready. They'll be here any second.

(*She prepares for the knitting group. He sits there.*)

BOB: Oh. Oh, great. I feel good now.

LIZ: Well, what kind of a question is that?

BOB: It's a perfectly legitimate question between two people who have been doing the things we do, Lizzie; might I remind you –

LIZ: What am I supposed to say? If I say, yes, I love you, then it's like I'm saying go ahead, dump my sister and ruin her life, and if I say no, then I'm just a terrible person who's doing all this because she hates her sister and wants to ruin her life. I mean, of course I love you, Bob, you're my best friend, but this is a mess! We have to stop, we just – oh. My life is – you know, I was supposed to have written a fucking novel by now. Or at least, a fucking book review for the Village Voice or something. But what am I doing? I'm interviewing complete morons for People magazine and having an affair with my sister's husband. I have to get back on track, Bob.

BOB: We will! We'll get a dog, move to Vermont, and grow maple syrup.

(*He puts his arms around her. She pulls away.*)

LIZ: You better go. She shouldn't find you here.

(*Pause. She cleans. He watches her.*)

BOB: You know, she knows.

LIZ: What?

BOB: I said, she knows. And you know she knows.

LIZ: What are you talking about? Did you tell her?

BOB: Of course not.

LIZ: Did she say something to you?

BOB: No.

LIZ: Then what are you talking about?

BOB: I'm just saying. She knows. I think she knew even before we started.

LIZ: Bob, we can't do this now . . .

BOB: It was that picnic, remember? She and Adelaide were wearing those matching dresses with little polka dots all over them, I always hate it when they do that, but they love wearing those matching dresses. And they were unpacking that perfect little basket, with the little deviled eggs that no one eats, and I looked over at you, and you were scratching a mosquito bite, and you were the only person there I felt related to at all. I looked back at Lily. And she was watching me, watch you. And there was something in her face. You know? Then that night . . .

LIZ: Is that why we started? I thought it was because you didn't get tenure.

(*Pause. He looks at her.*)

BOB: Never mind.

LIZ: Bob, come on, I'm just trying to –

BOB: I know what you are trying to do. And I'm just telling you. She knows.

(*They look at each other. Bob looks away, angry. After a moment, Liz crosses and touches him on the arm.*)

LIZ: I'm sorry. Hey, I'm sorry, it's just – when we started this, I thought it was the most real thing in my life, but now, I'm not so sure. I mean, we can't just – what are we going to do, run off? Neither of us has any money.

BOB: I thought money wasn't important to you.

LIZ: It is when I don't have it.

BOB: So, underneath it all, you're just like Lily, is that it?

LIZ: Oh. That was mean. That was really –

(*He grins at her. She shoves him, affectionate. They end up in an embrace.*)

LIZ: All right. You want to tell her? Let's tell her.

BOB: What?

LIZ: If she knows anyway, let's just admit it. If it's either that or getting caught, what's the point? Let's tell her.

BOB: You sure?

LIZ: Soon as she gets here.

BOB: Tonight? You want to tell her tonight?

LIZ: That's what you said.

BOB: It's – it's your knitting night.

LIZ: So?

BOB: I just – come on. It seems to me that there's gotta be a better time.

LIZ: A better time to say I want to divorce you to be with your sister, who I've been screwing for six months? What time would that be? Over brunch?

BOB: Maybe.

LIZ: Bob! You've been hoping she'd catch us for weeks! What's with the sudden obsession with protocol?

BOB: I just think there's no need to be cruel! I mean, I do have a little girl to think about!

(*Liz looks at him, stunned.*)

LIZ: Forget it. Really, Forget it.

BOB: Lizzie, we'll do it. I just want to do it right.

LIZ: No. We're not doing anything. There's nothing to do. We're not doing anything, ever again.

LOOSE KNIT
by Theresa Rebeck

Serio-Comic / 1 Man, 1 Woman
Paula & Miles: a couple on a blind date, 30s

The Setting: a sushi restaurant, the present

Here, two wildly different people suffer through a nightmare blind date.

PAULA: I've never seen them do that before.

MILES: Excuse me?

PAULA: I've never seen a waiter serve sushi like that. Like an offering. It's quite – remarkable.

MILES: I know. It's a little embarrassing. They call it the Imperial Feast, and the show comes with it. Sort of like those waiters who sing to you in pizza joints.

PAULA: I didn't think you went to pizza joints.

MILES: I don't. I come here.
(*He starts to serve her.*)

PAULA: I hope you don't mind my asking, but don't you find this all a bit . . . overstated?

MILES: Don't you like sushi? I love sushi.

PAULA: That's not what I meant. It's just, most people I know would be uncomfortable with the politics of all this. I mean, I've had a wonderful time tonight; meeting the governor was really exciting, and the opening at the Whitney was nothing short of dazzling. But to tell the truth, I'm beginning to find this all a little unnerving.

MILES: Really? How so?

PAULA: Well, you know, all of it together is so – all right. Your air of patronage, the subservience of everyone in the restaurant, your car – I mean don't you guys read the newspaper? This sort of thing is going out of style.

MILES: Do you really think so?

PAULA: Yes. I do.

MILES: I think you'd be surprised. The imperialistic structures which seem to disturb you so much have stood at the heart of the American culture for centuries. In fact, these structures, and the assumptions they are built upon, are the very things which have made culture possible. In America and throughout the world.

PAULA: Well, that may be, but –

MILES: Here, I think you'll appreciate this; it's a combination of abalone, salmon roe and mahi mahi. Only two people in the world know how to make it. It's exquisite, really.

PAULA: Thank you.

(*He places it on her plate and hands it to her, then makes a note in his notebook. As he interviews her, he continues to make notes.*)

PAULA: What are you doing?

MILES: Just making a few notes to myself, that's all. It's a business habit. Annoying but harmless. I picked it up from my father.

PAULA: (*Friendly.*) Really? What was he like?

MILES: No, no, no. I was warned about this. You're famous for this. No prying about my parents until the second date.

PAULA: You can't blame a girl for trying.

MILES: (*Laughing.*) I hope you don't mind my saying so, Paula, but this is the first time I've dated a woman of color. I find it quite stimulating.

PAULA: Really?

MILES: Don't you think so?

PAULA: Well, I've dated white men before.

MILES: So the novelty's worn off.

PAULA: I guess.

MILES: (*He writes this down.*) Do you have many white friends?

PAULA: Yes. Do you?

MILES: Well, it's less of an issue for me, isn't it?

PAULA: You tell me.

MILES: (*Laughing.*) Therapists. All I meant was, clearly, it's important for blacks to assimilate themselves into the high culture. Which you seem to have accomplished admirably.

PAULA: What?

MILES: An attractive black woman achieves a position of authority in a predominantly white profession? That looks like assimilation to me.

PAULA: Yes, well, just for the record, I'm not particularly interested in being assimilated into the "high" culture.

MILES: You're not?

PAULA: No. Most of my "friends" are black. And, as you may or may not realize, my family is black. You might want to write that down, too.

MILES: Do you see them often?

PAULA: Yes. I do.

MILES: How often?

PAULA: Often enough.

MILES: And your "black friends?" How often do you see them?

PAULA: I don't keep track of how often I –

MILES: And your white friends? How often do you see them?

PAULA: Often.

MILES: More often than you see your black friends?

PAULA: (*Pause, cold.*) Maybe.

MILES: That's the beauty of America, isn't it? Social mobility.
    (*He writes this down.*)

PAULA: Okay. What's going on here?

MILES: We're trying to get to know each other.

PAULA: Is that what we're doing?

MILES: Don't you want to know me, Paula? Because I find you fascinating.

PAULA: You're pretty fascinating yourself, Miles.

MILES: Thank you. So. You're a psychologist. How many patients do you have?
    (*Beat. Cautiously, Paula decides to answer.*)

PAULA: They're not patients, they're clients.

MILES: White?

PAULA: Would it make a difference if they were?

MILES: You tell me. You're the one who doesn't want to be assimilated.

PAULA: (*Pause.*) Yes. Most of them are white.

MILES: Do you like them?

PAULA: What is that supposed to mean?

MILES: It's a simple question.

PAULA: No, it's not.

MILES: I was just wondering how it felt to have white people come in and complain to you all the time.

PAULA: It feels just fine.

MILES: I think you're being coy.

PAULA: And I think you're attacking me.

MILES: I'm just trying to get to know you, Paula. And I really am interested in the whole therapeutic enterprise.

PAULA: Then maybe you should try it. I know a couple of people who might be able to help you with this notebook thing.

MILES: (*Smiling a little.*) I'll think about it. So, how long, on the average, do you work with any given client? One year? Two? Five? Ten?

PAULA: Yes.

MILES: Have they gotten better?

PAULA: Oh, my God . . .

MILES: Is that a delicate question? I'm sorry. I just don't understand why someone would need your services for ten years. I mean, it's a treatment, right? What good is a treatment if it doesn't make you better?

PAULA: (*Steely.*) Well, Miles, some people have been terribly damaged by life. Their souls have been – wounded, whether by their family, or events, or just the world –

MILES: Well, Paula, I'm sure you're good at what you do, but I'm not convinced that talking to you is going to heal my soul or even make me a successful member of society. I've just never understood why anyone thinks that discussing their problems will make them go away.

PAULA: No one thinks that.

MILES: Don't they?

PAULA: No.

MILES: I thought they did.

PAULA: Well, and so what if they do? Sometimes we all need someone to talk to just to – to get a perspective on things. The world's a hard place. Once in a while, even the best of us needs an ear, and a little shot of compassion. Is that so awful?

MILES: But you don't provide compassion. You provide a service.

PAULA: I also provide compassion.

MILES: If you require a person to pay for it, is it still compassion?

PAULA: Why are you attacking me?

MILES: Why do you see this as an attack? On the contrary, I have nothing but admiration for the shrewdness of your whole enterprise. You convince people they're dependent on you for their happiness, then you charge them for that dependency. It's brilliant.

PAULA: That is not what I do!

MILES: Of course not. I'm sorry if I touched a nerve. (*He writes.*) Have you tried the eel?

PAULA: No.

MILES: You should. (*Pause.*) Go ahead, try it. (*Pause.*) Try it.
(*She reaches for it. He smiles.*)

PAULA: All right, Miles. All right. I think we've talked about me quite enough for one evening. I'd like to hear about you. Why don't you tell me what kind of dreams you have?

MILES: You're interested in my dreams?

PAULA: Very.

MILES: (*Pause.*) All right. (*Pause.*) There's one I have where I'm in my office above the city, and there's a document in the computer that I can't get out. So I look in my desk for the key to the computer and it looks like a knife, or a letter opener; it's quite sharp, but just as I'm about to put it into the computer a white rat comes along and steals it out of my hand. So I chase her up and down the halls, and then I hear her behind me, so I turn, and hold out my hand, and the knife is in it – the key, I mean – but it's a different rat, a black rat, only now she's covered in blood because I've stabbed her. Because I had the key all along. (*Pause.*) Actually, I've had that dream several times.

PAULA: Really.

MILES: Do you know what it means?

PAULA: No. No. I have no idea.
(*She stares at him. Blackout.*)

NORTH EAST LOCAL
by Tom Donaghy

Dramatic / 1 Man, 1 Woman
  Mickey & Gi: an estranged couple, 50s

The Setting: the home of Mickey and Gi

Mickey and Gi have been separated for many years. Here they reunite briefly for the sale of the house they had once believed they would grow old in – together.

○　　　○　　　○

GI: You want anything?

MICKEY: Nuh.

GI: Some root beer? Got some sitting there for the movers.

MICKEY: Fine, nuh.

GI: You want it you're just not saying it. (*Goes, and from off.*) The little cards I'm doing are in all the stores. A man came into the shop a month or so ago, a distributor and I had them laying out, and he bought them. The *idea* he bought.

MICKEY: How bout it.

GI: And a factory makes them now. So they're all over in the stores and people call me up. (*Re-enters with root beer.*) So there's money too – for the first time. And I'm going to Paris. Paris, France, Mick.

MICKEY: That's great, Gi.

GI: The cards have little animals on them. Maybe I showed you one once?

MICKEY: Don't think so.

GI: There're little sayings on them some other person writes like: "On your birthday, have a bear of a time." That's not a good one. There's one I like that says: "Don't be a chicken, give me a call sometime." Guess that's not so hot either. They wanted me to make one with squirrels and I – I put my foot down. I went, "No squirrels! You should see what they did to our roof."

MICKEY: You tell people something like that and they look at you like you got two heads!

GI: They think you're crazy. But apparently the cards're "moving." That's what they say, "moving." Guess that means they're going places. They really are communicating with people all over the place. So many people and me are connected. (*Pause.*) I still don't have any girlfriends, though. Most women have girlfriends.

MICKEY: Busy s'all.

GI: I'da liked a grandchild. I'd like that for Stef. Cause there's still time. And today people have all kinds of options, like adopting, and well, just all kinds of options you and me never even –. Cause no one gets married anymore anyway. Think you get married as like an insurance thing that you hope there's gonna be someone at the end. Think that's the cruelest thing we do to people. But's hard not to be cruel so much of the time. Should just marry them cause they bother us less than most people.

MICKEY: (*Pulls a strand out of her brush.*) What's this?

GI: It's my hair.

MICKEY: But it's silver.

GI: It's from the rinse. My hairdresser said if I kept dying it, they'd fall out eventually, imagine? So he just rinses it out with a little color so there's silver coming through.

MICKEY: Just little.

GI: I'm fifty-two.

MICKEY: 'Snuthin.

GI: Coulda gone bald! (*Pause.*) We're simple people. We wanted simple things –

MICKEY: Shh.

GI: (*Pause.*) The couple who's moving in's from Manayunk. She said they could make use of the wreck room. Didn't ask her for what. I told her to go ahead and try, we never knew what to do with it.

MICKEY: Ah you know, they get ideas.

GI: Uh-uh.

MICKEY: New marrieds have all kindsa ideas bout a new place.

GI: They aren't even married.

MICKEY: Kids today, right – Probably won't recognize if we ever drive by.

GI: New train won't even stop here, express only, city to city. The house'll be like a blurry speck when you go by. No one'd even know anyone lived here they'd be going by so fast. I'm always wondering what's the hurry?

MICKEY: Always a bus man myself.

GI: Just the house is too big for just me.

MICKEY: Always felt bad it was small.

GI: It was. Now it's too big. (*Pause.*) The movers're here.

MICKEY: Maybe when you get settled a cup of coffee, or –

GI: (*Pause.*) I'd like that.

MICKEY: Look. (*Pointing.*) Rhododendron got their flowers.

GI: Lining the walk.

MICKEY: Spring is what.

GI: We planted them.

MICKEY: Spring's what it is.

GI: Who'da even noticed, all that's been going on?

ONE-EYED VENUS AND THE BROTHERS
by Le Wilhelm

Serio-Comic / 1 Man, 1 Woman
Rufus: a devoted fisherman, 30-40
Patch: the woman he loves, 30-40

The Setting: the bank of the James River, Missouri Ozarks, 1959

Rufus has decided to see to it that his handicapped younger brother, Ron, should lose his virginity. To that end he appeals to Patch, an earthy woman who has been his friend since childhood, to grant him this very special favor.

O   O   O

PATCH: (*Walking toward the river.*) That'd be a rough one for me. (*Smiles, listening to the water.*) Damn rough. One of these days I'm going to paint her. One of these days.
RUFUS: How's that coming?
PATCH: Painting?
RUFUS: Mmmh.
PATCH: Good. Real good.
RUFUS: Mmmh.
PATCH: Sold six of my canvases to a gallery down in Tulsa. Not making me rich, but I'm supporting myself. Got enough left over to buy a little grub for you guys. You know something?
RUFUS: Mmmh?
PATCH: Going to paint you one of these days.
RUFUS: Hell.
PATCH: Am.
RUFUS: What you want to paint an ornery cuss like me for?
PATCH: Loco.
(*She laughs, he laughs.*)
You and this river. Like to paint this river showing all the things that have happened. Be like one of them autobiographies. Paint it all.
RUFUS: I know one night you'd better not paint.

PATCH: That's exactly one of the things I would paint.

RUFUS: Hell.

PATCH: The spirit of it, Rufus. The spirit, not the actual goings-on. Paint all them things, little boys fishing on this river bank late at night. Sitting on the bank huddled close together, waiting for a big ol' fish to bite. Pretty soon they'll be touching each other, helping each other squirt their first drops right here on this river bank.

RUFUS: You're crazy.

PATCH: Oh hell, Rufus, what kids do when they're growing up. If you didn't you was the exception, not the rule. Paint all that. Time I grabbed a noodling hook and went down to that old flat rock that's down around the bend, stuck that hook way down in the hole and hooked me a big old yellow cat. Forty pounder. Did it by myself. Nigh on to tore my arm off. I want to paint all that, Rufus.

RUFUS: You'll get thrown in the county jail for painting some of that stuff.

PATCH: (*Harshly.*) What'd you want me here for, Rufus? Just auld lang syne? To be with you and your brothers?

RUFUS: You're important to me, Patch.

PATCH: Mmmh.

RUFUS: Don't you know that?

PATCH: Yeah, I know.

RUFUS: Just thought –

PATCH: Rufus, cut the malarkey. What do you want?

RUFUS: (*Laughs.*) Patch.

PATCH: Mmmh.

RUFUS: I was wondering –

PATCH: Yeah?

RUFUS: It's Ron.

PATCH: Ron?

RUFUS: Yeah, Ron. Seeing as how you played such an im-

PATCH: (*Knowing.*) Ah.

RUFUS: I was wondering if you'd . . .

PATCH: Yeah?

RUFUS: If you'd do it with Ron.

PATCH: I see.

RUFUS: Like you did with me and the rest of my brothers.

PATCH: Mmmh.

RUFUS: I'd really appreciate it.

PATCH: You would?

RUFUS: Yes, I would. Seeing as how he's had polio and all. He needs . . . . make him into a man.

PATCH: Ah.

RUFUS: Yeah.

PATCH: You think if I did it with him it'd make your little brother into a man?

RUFUS: Yes, I do.

PATCH: Hell, Rufus, I might possess strange healing powers.

RUFUS: What are you talking about?

PATCH: You say that having sex with me can turn a boy into a man, maybe I got some kind of special healing powers, Rufus. Like Reverend Glidewell when he lays on hands. Maybe if Ron and I do it, all of the crippling effects of polio will just go and disappear?

RUFUS: I don't think it'd do that, Patch, but I think it'd be real good for him.

PATCH: Don't you think a roll in the hay with me will cure his polio?

RUFUS: Damn it, this is serious, Patch! He's a good kid. Hell, you know how women are around these parts.

PATCH: No, I don't. Why don't you tell me?

RUFUS: They ain't going to be doing it with him. You might be the only one that ever will.

PATCH: So you think I'm the only woman around here who don't think enough of herself, don't respect herself enough, so I'll do it with him.

RUFUS: You're twisting things around on me. You always do that. You didn't do that when you were young. But you went away to college and you learned how to twist everything around.

PATCH: Then why don't you untwist it for me, Rufus?

RUFUS: I'm saying that you're different, Patch.

PATCH: I understood that.

RUFUS: That you can see past a man's outside and into his heart.

PATCH: Well, I'm really something special, ain't I?

RUFUS: This is very important!!!

PATCH: Rufus, how paralyzed is he?

RUFUS: What do you mean?

PATCH: He might not even be able to.

RUFUS: (*Flaring.*) Hell he can't!

PATCH: I thought you said he hadn't ever.

RUFUS: He can, though.

PATCH: He can?

RUFUS: (*Angry.*) Damn straight he can!!

PATCH: Just asked!

RUFUS: Just told!

PATCH: (*Curious, but reserved.*) How do you know?

RUFUS: 'Bout a year ago, we had some folks from Arkansas. Whole raft of 'em. Boys and girls. I saw Ron take off. Got to thinking he was upset 'cause he couldn't do some of the stuff that . . . anyways, I followed him . . . found him out behind the cowbarn sitting on that big ol' flat rock with his lizard out, just –

PATCH: (*Incredulous.*) His what?

RUFUS: Lizard. His lizard.

PATCH: His lizard?

RUFUS: Yeah.

PATCH: Is that what you call it?

RUFUS: That's what grandma always called it . . . you know what I'm talking about.

PATCH: Reckon I do.

RUFUS: Look, Patch, it's awful important to me. He's the last of my brothers. I'd be beholden to you.

PATCH: Rufus, I've done it for a lot of reasons in my life, but I'm getting old. Just 'bout past the age of having any young'n's. Always wanted one. Just one. Getting too old to be doing things as favors. They take their toll when I ain't getting nothing.

RUFUS: Who says you ain't going to be getting nothing. He's big.

PATCH: Ah.

RUFUS: Bigger than me.

PATCH: (*Amused.*) Is that a fact?

RUFUS: Yeah. Surprised me.

PATCH: And since your brother has this big . . . lizard, that's going to do something special for me?

RUFUS: Well, sure . . . I figured –

PATCH: You did?

RUFUS: Mmmh.

PATCH: Uh.

RUFUS: Course, I've heard that some women like to reach for them.

PATCH: Rufus, you've still got a lot to learn.

PLAY WITH REPEATS
by Martin Crimp

Dramatic / 1 Man, 1 Woman
   Tony: a man living parts of his life over again, 30s
   Heather: the woman he desires, 30s

The Setting: a city, the present

Tony has been given the dubious gift of living parts of his life over again. Here, he reencounters Heather, a woman he believes he once lost because he wasn't aggressive enough the first time he met her.

(*A temporary bus-stop. Night. Tony stands holding his present. Also waiting is a woman of similar age. They exchange a brief glance and smile. Silence. When their eyes meet again they begin to speak.*)

WOMAN: Are you waiting for –

TONY: A three-three-nine, that's right.
   (*Both faint laugh.*)

TONY: We may as well sleep here.

WOMAN: I'm sorry? (*Faint laugh.*) Yes.

TONY: Joke.

WOMAN: I know. I'm sorry.

TONY: No, I'm sorry.

WOMAN: No, you're right. You're absolutely right. It's only you meet . . .

TONY: I frightened you.

WOMAN: No, it's only you meet . . . Sometimes late at night . . .

TONY: You can meet some pretty weird people late at night.

WOMAN: Yes.
   (*Both faint laugh.*)
   I don't know why they had to move the stop somewhere so dark.

TONY: It's only temporary.

WOMAN: D'you think it will be permanently like this? Some friends from the Institute were meant to be giving me a lift, but –

TONY: But they buggered off.

WOMAN: How did you guess?

(*Both faint laugh.*)

No really . . .

TONY: Human nature . . .

WOMAN: . . . how did you know that?

TONY: What Institute is that? Is that the –

WOMAN: I go to classes there. Crossley Road.

TONY: Uh-hu.

WOMAN: I'm involved in various things.

TONY: Uh-hu. Is that right.

So what sort of things are various things?

WOMAN: Well, for example, there's History.

TONY: That's fascinating.

WOMAN: This term it's the twentieth century.

TONY: No, that's fascinating. The twentieth century. That's . . .

WOMAN: (*Dispassionate list.*) Vietnam. The Holocaust. The Atom Bomb, of course. Then we go back to the Spanish Civil War. Guernica. And of course we've done the Somme, the battle of the Somme . . .

TONY: That's a picture, isn't it?

WOMAN: Sorry?

TONY: Guernica is a picture.

WOMAN: Is it?

Of course Lawrence uses a lot of visual material. Photographs. Films.

TONY: Lawrence being . . .

WOMAN: Lawrence is our tutor.

TONY: So, what, you memorize . . .

WOMAN: Memorize?

TONY: Memorize the dates.

WOMAN: We try to memorize the dates. But Lawrence doesn't really like us doing that. He's very keen on making us think. He says he doesn't care if we've been working all day long, we still mustn't accept what's happened without thinking about why. Why why why. He gets quite angry. (*Faint laugh.*) He's actually quite attractive.

TONY: Is he?

WOMAN: You might've heard of him. Bott. Lawrence Bott.

TONY: Lawrence Bott.

No. (*Vague recollection.*) No, actually it is familiar.

WOMAN: He's just published a book.

TONY: So what's he been getting angry about tonight?

WOMAN: Tonight? No. Sorry. Tonight was French. Tuesday's is French.

TONY: Right. Bonjour Mademoiselle.

(*Both faint laugh.*)

WOMAN: What's that?

TONY: It's French.

WOMAN: I know, but what does it mean?

TONY: Bonjour Mademoiselle? Well it's . . . hello. It just means hello.

WOMAN: We haven't done that yet. What we're doing this term is we're just making the sounds. It has some beautiful sounds.

TONY: The language of love.

WOMAN: You don't go –

TONY: To classes? No, but . . .

WOMAN: But I suppose you have interests.

TONY: Well what interests me is human nature.

WOMAN: Human nature is fascinating.

TONY: Because you can go to classes. That's one way and I respect that. But the other way is to sit tight. You observe. You compare. You don't do anything as such. But you analyze. You analyze and over the years you find that what you accumulate . . .

WOMAN: Is wisdom.

TONY: Yes.

(*Both smile. Tony's increasing self-confidence has a mesmerizing effect on the woman.*)

Hold this a minute. (*He gives her the present.*)

WOMAN: D'you know who you're like; you're very like Lawrence.

TONY: Am I?

(*He presses his fingers to his temples.*)

WOMAN: (*Amused.*) What're you doing?

TONY: Heather.

WOMAN: How d'you know that?

TONY: Heather. Your name is Heather.

WOMAN: How did you do that?

(*Tony laughs.*)

WOMAN: (*Laughs.*) No, how did you do that?

TONY: Heather. That's your name.

WOMAN: Yes.

TONY: Your name is Heather.

WOMAN: I know. Yes. Are you psychic?

TONY: What's mine?

WOMAN: (*Laughs.*) I've no idea.

TONY: You don't know my name?

WOMAN: No. Are you famous?

TONY: Anthony. Anthony Steadman. No, I'm not famous.

WOMAN: Well hello, Anthony.

TONY: Hello, Heather.

> (*They laugh and shake hands. Heather moves away, rubbing her bare arms. Silence. Then.*)

HEATHER: Have I met you somewhere?

TONY: You're cold. (*He takes off his jacket.*)

HEATHER: No, it's nothing.

TONY: No, you're cold. Your arms are cold. Come on.

> (*Heather acquiesces and he helps her into the jacket.*)
>
> It's because the sky's clear, It gets cold when the sky's clear.

HEATHER: I must look like an idiot in this . . . Some kind of scarecrow. (*Laughing she 'models' the jacket.*)

TONY: No. fantastic. You look fantastic.

HEATHER: What is this anyway?

> (*i.e., the present which she holds.*)

TONY: You really do.

HEATHER: What is this?

TONY: For you. Open it.

HEATHER: But it's yours.

TONY: No. Go on. Open it.

> (*She starts to unwrap.*)
>
> It suits you.
>
> You see there are two things. One, it's my birthday. Two, I've been promoted.

HEATHER: I think someone's had this before you. It's half empty.

TONY: What?

HEATHER: I said I think someone's –

TONY: Yes I heard you. What d'you mean?

HEATHER: Look.

(*Tony takes the bottle, which is less than half-full.*)
So . . . it sounds like you've got a lot to celebrate.
TONY: What's this supposed to mean?
HEATHER: Congratulations.
TONY: I mean is this supposed to be some kind of a comment?
HEATHER: Someone's made a mistake, that's all.
TONY: Terry.
HEATHER: That's not something you could do intentionally.
TONY: Because Terry can keep it.
HEATHER: It's not important is it?
TONY: No. I'm sorry.
HEATHER: Terry. Is that . . . is that a girl's name?
TONY: A girl? No. Terry . . . how would you describe Terry? He's just . . . one of my employees. We're obliged you see to take on a certain number of mentally handicapped people.
HEATHER: That's very humane.
TONY: Yes.
(*Silence. Then both faint laugh.*)
Look in the pockets.
HEATHER: What?
TONY: No, have a look. (*She feels in the jacket pockets, while he opens the bottle.*) This time I'm prepared.
(*Heather discovers two paper cups. She laughs.*)
HEATHER: Did you *plan* this? You know, I don't normally drink spirits.
TONY: (*Pouring drinks.*) Neither do I. I drink lager as a rule, premium lager. Cheers.
HEATHER: Cheers. To us.
TONY: To us.
(*Both drink. Tony immediately refills his cup.*)
HEATHER: Have I met you somewhere?
TONY: You've never married.
HEATHER: Sorry?
TONY: You've never –
HEATHER: No. Married? No.
TONY: I haven't.
HEATHER: Is that a matter of principle?
TONY: Absolutely not. No.
HEATHER: You see I'm not against marriage. But interestingly enough that's an area where Lawrence and I, we part

company. Because Lawrence, he's a very right-on sort of person, and –

TONY: What's that? What's right-on?

HEATHER: Well it means . . . I suppose it means he's basically to the left . . .

TONY: Un-hu . . .

HEATHER: And as someone who is basically to the left – which I respect him for that – but he feels that a woman shouldn't let herself be defined –

TONY: This is what Lawrence feels . . .

HEATHER: Yes. Shouldn't let herself – historically speaking – be defined in terms of her sexual role, i.e. wife, mistress, mother. He says it's degrading. And in our class we have these discussions where we clash. (*Faint laugh.*) Lawrence and I always clash, because I say to him –

TONY: Right. (*He takes the bottle.*)

HEATHER: Look, Lawrence, a woman can't turn her back on her sexuality any more than a man can. She can't become neutral. Because isn't neutrality equally degrading? You can't ignore what you biologically are. (*As Tony refills her cup.*) Just a little. But Lawrence disputes that. (*Faint laugh.*) I think – although of course I shouldn't say this – but I think perhaps he has an ethnic problem.

(*Silence. Heather wraps the jacket around herself.*)

This is warm. Thank you.

Did you read that thing?

TONY: What thing is that?

HEATHER: It was just a thing. I read this thing where two tourists, there were two tourists, on a beach, it was on a Greek island, this is a crowded beach, and what they did was they just started to make love, I mean in front of everyone, on a crowded beach.

TONY: That's offensive.

HEATHER: But I don't think that it *is*, Anthony. You see I think we have to admit what we biologically are. That some things may simply be inevitable. But of course Lawrence disputes that. (*She drinks.*) And it's the same with children.

TONY: I like children.

HEATHER: So do I. I love them, because they're innocent and they're the future. But Lawrence won't hear about the future.

He says: look at the world, what right do we have to a future? And each week he turns out the lights and he shows us films: cities in ruins, or human bodies being bulldozed into graves. Which is all very well. Which is all very well but we still have a right. Because each generation, each child, is another life. Is a chance to escape from that.

TONY: I know exactly what you mean.

HEATHER: Just because one generation, one life, has failed, doesn't mean that the next one will. That's not logical.

TONY: No.

HEATHER: And besides I think we all as human beings have a duty to direct people's attention away from all that ugliness.

TONY: I know. There's this Complex at the back of us, it takes away all the light . . .

HEATHER: Exactly. architecture.

(*She drinks. Confidential.*) You see – personally – I don't believe that number of people died. In the gas chambers. I don't believe it's *humanly possible* for that number of people to die.

TONY: I don't believe it either. I never have.

HEATHER: It can't be.

Which isn't to trivialize. You see, Anthony, I think that if – like Lawrence – if you stare at ugly things for long enough, you get ugly yourself, inside. We need to show people the beautiful things. Those are the things we need to show to our children.

TONY: We need to wake up.

HEATHER: Wake up. That's beautiful. Yes.

Shall I tell you what I really like? I really like visiting stately homes. I've got a kind of season ticket and at the weekends I take off to a stately home . . .

TONY: Woburn Abbey . . .

HEATHER: The big ones naturally. But also when you apply you get a list of all the smaller ones nobody knows. So mostly it's those I visit. And that's the most beautiful thing. The most beautiful thing is to sit in one of those rooms and imagine it's mine. The plasterwork, the marble fireplaces, the gilding. Things that've lasted for hundreds of years. Mahogany floors. Do you think that's wrong?

TONY: No.

HEATHER: No it's not wrong. I know it's not wrong because I feel at home there, Anthony. What it is is a sense of confidence, of order. I can breathe. I say to myself: yes, this is me. You walk out in the gardens and what strikes you is the symmetry. Boxwood hedges. Pineapples made of stone. Round the walls there are fruit trees growing along wires. Figs. Morello cherries. Plums. In some of them they're recreating the past exactly. They're growing the same plants . . . the same species of plants. In the same places. As they were then. The same trees.

TONY: That's extraordinary.

HEATHER: So not just the house but the whole landscape is as it would've been. (*She drinks.*) I'm not making myself clear.

TONY: You are. Yes, you are. Landscapes. That's exactly how it should be.

HEATHER: And it makes me think, it makes me think, Anthony, that if we would wear those clothes . . .

TONY: Uh-hu . . .

HEATHER: Or speak, speak as they did . . .

TONY: Like a person of that time . . . Speak poetry . . .

HEATHER: Because don't you ever get the feeling that the words we use . . .

TONY: We can't express ourselves . . .

HEATHER: . . . that the words we use are just the shadow of a language that we've lost. And perhaps if we could speak that language . . .

TONY: I know . . .

HEATHER: Speak poetry . . . Or dance . . .

TONY: Yes . . .

HEATHER: They could all dance . . . (*She puts down her cup and offers her hand.*) Come on.

TONY: What?

HEATHER: We can dance.

TONY: Dance.

HEATHER: Yes. Come on.

TONY: You mean dance. You mean actually dance? Now?

HEATHER: I mean actually dance. yes.

TONY: (*Faint laugh.*) I can't.

HEATHER: You can. (*She takes his hand.*) Of course you can. Why should we be limited by preconceived ideas about ourselves?

(*They begin to dance, without close physical contact, oddly graceful. Heather repeatedly hums a short slow phrase, and Tony joins in this ostinato. Time passes before Heather speaks.*)

In summer they have concerts. They play music on the old instruments, the original instruments.

(*They continue to dance and hum.*)

Perhaps that's where we met.

TONY: Where?

HEATHER: In one of those houses, one of those rooms. In a previous life.

(*Both faint laugh. The dance continues until Tony breaks gently away.*)

TONY: I need a piss.

(*They both laugh. While Tony finds a dark corner, Heather, still humming the tune, leans against a wall.*)

HEATHER: Bonjour Mademoiselle. (*Faint laugh.*)

(*She continues to hum.. Tony returns into the light. He drains the bottle into his mouth. Taking the bottle he goes to Heather and presses himself against her.*)

TONY: Let's do it.

HEATHER: What are you doing?

TONY: Come on. Let's do it.

HEATHER: What're you talking about?

(*It takes a moment for Heather to realize that Tony is in earnest. But there is no question of an ambiguous response: she is utterly terrified.*)

Get off me. What're you doing?

TONY: Shut up. Let's just do it.

HEATHER: Oh Jesus Christ.

TONY: Come on.

HEATHER: SOMEBODY HELP ME!

(*They struggle.*)

TONY: Come on. Ease up. Relax. (*He pins her against the wall.*) Come on. Pull this up. Help me. Pull it up. You're not helping me.

HEATHER: Oh Christ you're ripping . . . Help me, he's insane.

TONY: You see the mistake I made last time . . . I frightened you by being weak. I'm sorry.

HEATHER: Just fuck off of me, fuck off . . .

TONY: I respected you as a *person* . . .

HEATHER: Help me . . .

TONY: What I failed to see last time was that – KEEP STILL – was that I needed to assert myself . . .

HEATHER: What d'you mean last time? What d'you mean?

TONY: But this time. Look. I'm in control. Ease up, Heather. Relax. Pull this up . . .

HEATHER: Please. It's a mistake . . .

TONY: I love you. I'm in control . . .

HEATHER: Look, you're confusing me with someone. We've never met . . .

TONY: No no no. You don't understand . . .

HEATHER: I do. I do understand, Anthony. Yes if we could just think about this, if we could just decide, just decide who it is –

TONY: KEEP STILL CAN'T YOU FUCK YOU!
(*He smashes the bottle against the wall. Heather turns her head away in terror and closes her eyes, too afraid of the glass to fight. This sudden passivity confuses Tony.*)
What's wrong? Your eyes are shut. What's wrong?

HEATHER: Just do it. Please, please don't hurt me. Just do it. Just do it and go away.

TONY: What d'you mean?

HEATHER: (*Eyes shut.*) I haven't seen you. I swear I can't describe you. Don't hurt me.

TONY: What d'you mean? We've been talking. We've been dancing. What d'you mean you can't describe me?
(*Heather cannot speak.*)
Open your eyes. OPEN YOUR EYES! (*He drops the piece of bottle and forces her eyes open.*) Look. It's me. Don't you remember me? This is me. Anthony. I want to marry you. We're going to have children.
(*Heather spits in his face.*)

TONY: You don't mean that. I'm sorry but you don't mean that. Yes yes yes last time we missed our chance, and perhaps you feel strongly, but now it's different. I'm in control.
(*Heather slips away.*)
Or we could have a meal.
We could have a meal. We could talk.
(*Blackout.*)

SNAKEBIT
by David Marshall Grant

Dramatic / 1 Man, 1 Woman
   Jonathan: a self-centered actor, 30-40
   Jennifer: his wife, 30-40

The Setting: a house in Los Angeles, the present

Many years ago, Jennifer slept with Jonathan's best friend, Michael, who is gay. Now, she is terrified that her young daughter is infected with HIV. After mustering up the courage to be tested, she calls the lab for the results.

O   O   O

JENNIFER: Your fly's open, Jonathan.
JONATHAN: What?
JENNIFER: There, I said something.
JONATHAN: Fuck you. What do you mean my fly's open?
(*He stops, checks it, and pulls it up.*)
Are you crazy? You've been looking at my fly, open, all day?
JENNIFER: I was looking at your underwear.
JONATHAN: You sat at The Ivy and watched my underwear? What is going on with you? Are you sick? Do you have a fever?
JENNIFER: I don't want to talk to you anymore, Jonathan.
JONATHAN: You're crazy now.
JENNIFER: I'm terrified right now. I'm terrified.
JONATHAN: Why? And don't say I'm mean. I'm not mean. I'm just trying to get through the fucking day here.
JENNIFER: I'm not part of the day, I'm your wife.
JONATHAN: Right. Idiot! And if you would just act like one, make me feel good about myself, I wouldn't scream all the time. I am not going to be nice in Hollywood, California. I am in the real world. I am not going to apologize for that. I am not going to apologize for protecting myself.
JENNIFER: What difference does it make? There's nothing left of you to protect. You've killed everything in you worth saving.

You just attack. That's all you do. It's not self defense, it's war. You're the monster now, Jonathan, there's no bigger prick than you.

(*Beat.*)

And in case you haven't noticed, and I guess you haven't, I don't like standing in front of a lot of people and shaking. And that's what I do, I shake on stage, and sometimes I can't talk, which I guess you did notice. I stand there waiting for my lines to come and I can't get them out . . . and that can be a nightmare, that kind of doom; really, that's what it is, impending doom, and I don't want to feel that anymore . . . I slept with Michael. I had sex with him.

JONATHAN: You did what?

JENNIFER: You don't know me.

JONATHAN: You did what?

JENNIFER: I'm afraid Emma's sick. I've been worried since January.

JONATHAN: When did you sleep with Michael?

JENNIFER: I don't know anything. I took a test. That's all I know.

JONATHAN: (*Walking on eggshells.*) You took a test?

JENNIFER: Monday.

JONATHAN: Jennifer, is Michael . . . Do you know that Michael is . . . ?

JENNIFER: I don't know. We're supposed to call now.

JONATHAN: But Michael doesn't know he's sick?

JENNIFER: No. We're supposed to call them.

JONATHAN: So you both took a test?

JENNIFER: Yes.

JONATHAN: Because you thought it might be a possibility?

JENNIFER: Yes.

JONATHAN: And it's ready today?

JENNIFER: Yes.

JONATHAN: And you call them?

JENNIFER: Yes you call.

JONATHAN: And you find out.

JENNIFER: (*She gets up.*) Where's my purse? The number's in my purse. And a code. I have a code thing. L799 something. I need for you to go to the gym.

JONATHAN: Jennifer –

JENNIFER: I promised Michael we would call together. I need for you to go to the gym.

JONATHAN: Calm down.

JENNIFER: I am very calm. We took it together and we're going to call together.

JONATHAN: Jennifer, you're getting hysterical.

JENNIFER: I don't want you here when he comes back.

JONATHAN: Jennifer –

JENNIFER: I'm not hysterical.

JONATHAN: Jennifer.

JENNIFER: What?

JONATHAN: Will you listen to me?

JENNIFER: Oh God, I'm going to lose my mind.

JONATHAN: Can you just sit down?

JENNIFER: No.

JONATHAN: Fine. just listen then. I'm not going to the gym. Okay? I'm talking calmly right now, but inside I want you to know I am not calm, I am far from calm. Okay? I am glad you're calm, but I am not calm. Now, I just want you for a moment to consider what you're asking me to do. Okay, can you picture that? Okay. So you can understand why I'm not going to the gym? Okay?

JENNIFER: Yes, I understand. Stop patronizing me, I don't want you to patronize me.

JONATHAN: Fine. Can I ask you a question? You slept with Michael?

JENNIFER: Yes.

JONATHAN: When?

JENNIFER: In 1982.

JONATHAN: In 1982? And this is why you think Emma's sick? I don't think Michael was even sleeping with men in 1982.

JENNIFER: He did.

JONATHAN: But the doctors would have told us if they thought it was a possibility.

JENNIFER: Why? They didn't know all the information.

JONATHAN: But the chances –

JENNIFER: I know what the chances are.

JONATHAN: It's been ten years.

JENNIFER: It incubates –

JONATHAN: I know, but the chances –

JENNIFER: I know what the chances are.

(*Beat.*)

JONATHAN: We were married in 1982.

JENNIFER: It was before. Three months before.

JONATHAN: Alright, I don't think any of this is a problem. Okay? I think this has all been built up in your mind and before we all have a heart attack here I think we should just call. So give me the number.

JENNIFER: I'm waiting for Michael. I have to.

JONATHAN: (*Trying not to explode.*) Jesus fucking Christ. You know, I'm trying to be understanding, Jenny, I'm trying to do the right thing here, but you are making this almost impossible. Jennifer. I'm holding on to us by nothing. Do you understand? By less than nothing.

JENNIFER: If you want to stay here –

JONATHAN: This is my family! I'm about to snap, really I am. (*Trying to calm down.*)
Yes I want to stay here. I want you to call. That's what I want you to do. I just want you and I to make this call together. I'm your husband. Michael is not your husband. You had no right to sleep with him, Jenny. God damn you, it's just completely faithless.

JENNIFER: Please stop it, Jonathan.

JONATHAN: (*Exploding.*) NO, YOU STOP IT, GOD DAMN IT! I'M NOT DOING ANYTHING! OKAY? YOU'RE THE ONE WHO FUCKED HIM! I DIDN'T FUCK HIM! YOU FUCKED HIM! YOU FUCKED MY BEST FRIEND, JENNIFER! THAT'S COMPLETELY UNBELIEVABLE. HE'S MY BEST FRIEND. FUCK YOU! I COULD BE DEAD RIGHT NOW! FUCK YOU!
(*Beat. Jennifer crosses to the phone.*)
I'm sorry.
(*She says nothing, just starts to dial.*)
Jennifer, I'm sorry.

JENNIFER: Yes. Hello, I'm calling about . . . Pardon me? . . . Yes.

JONATHAN: Jennifer, I didn't mean it. Hang up.

JENNIFER: Yes, I'm calling about a test result . . .

JONATHAN: Hang up. Please hang up.

JENNIFER: (*To Jonathan.*)
What are you going to do if something happens right now?
(*Into the phone.*)
Hello . . . Yes, I'm holding.

JONATHAN: I lost control. Please, hang up. I love you, I don't want you to find this out right now.

JENNIFER: (*Into the phone.*)

Yes, hello . . . Yes I'm calling about a test result . . . Yes. L798. (*She checks the piece of paper.*)

No I'm sorry. L7998 . . . Yes, L7998 . . . I know it matters, that's why I'm saying it slowly and I don't need your attitude, okay. You're being critical and completely inappropriate. So just listen.

(*She says it very slowly.*)

L7998 . . . Thank you.

JONATHAN: Jennifer –

JENNIFER: (*To Jonathan.*)

No. Don't say anything.

(*Long pause. Then into the phone.*)

Yes . . . Oh. Okay. Thank you.

(*She slowly hangs up and stands there silently for a long time.*)

JONATHAN: Jennifer? Jennifer?

JENNIFER: I'm negative. I feel like I'm going to cry or something.

JONATHAN: Oh, God.

JENNIFER: You see your whole life.

JONATHAN: Come here. Sweetheart, come here.

JENNIFER: Flash before your eyes. Just like that.

JONATHAN: I'm sorry. Jenny. Jenny.

JENNIFER: And you realize what it is.

JONATHAN: Come here. Sweetheart?

JENNIFER: No.

STANTON'S GARAGE
by Joan Ackerman

Serio-Comic / 1 Man, 1 Woman
   Harlon: a gas station attendant, 17
   Frannie: a sheltered young lady, 16

The Setting: a service station in upstate Missouri, the present

Frannie and her stepmother-to-be are stranded when their Volvo breaks down in rural Missouri. Frannie winds up spending the day and evening with Harlon, a worker at the service station, and offers to pierce his ear for him.

(It is 4:00 a.m. The slightest bit of morning light should become visible during this scene. Frannie and Harlon enter with flashlight from stage right, carrying a sleeping bag and blanket; Harlon, dressed in his softball uniform, carries a small paper bag. Harlon reaches inside the outside garage door to turn on a light switch. Little overhead outside light on garage goes on.)

HARLON: *(Puts sown a sleeping bag.)* This here's your mattress. And . . . bed covers.

FRANNIE: Voila.

HARLON: You mind if I stay a minute or two?

FRANNIE: What do you mean, I'm going to do your ear, aren't I?

HARLON: I just didn't know if you'd mind me being in your bedroom. And all.

FRANNIE: It smells like manure.

HARLON: Mm. For Bonnie's tomatoes. She likes everything organic.

FRANNIE: Bonnie in Mexico?

HARLON: It's her garage. Inherited it from her daddy. Yeah, I've never been in a girl's bedroom before.

FRANNIE: Did she break the law?

HARLON: Broke a few laws. Broke a few hearts. There's a warrant out for her arrest.

FRANNIE: What did she do? Tell me.

HARLON: Six counts of fraud, for starters. Bait and switch. Regulation stuff. With the state, with her meters. Some woman sued her. Yeah, I've been in cars, movies, never a girl's bedroom.

FRANNIE: Why did the woman sue her?

HARLON: Bonnie sold her a set of tires she didn't need. Are you going with anyone?

FRANNIE: She sold her a set of tires she didn't need?

HARLON: Yeah, some New York bitch. Givin' Denny a hard time. Course Denny's too nice a guy to say anything.

FRANNIE: Were you honest with us?

HARLON: Huh?

FRANNIE: With Lee and me.

HARLON: Yeah.

FRANNIE: You honestly couldn't fix our car?

HARLON: Uh . . . we don't see too many Volvos.

FRANNIE: Well I'm glad. I didn't want to go to that wedding.

HARLON: Good. I knew that. Silvie had it fixed within an hour, I pulled a few wires. Just kidding. Do you have a boyfriend?

FRANNIE: No. Look.

HARLON: What?

FRANNIE: The moon.

HARLON: You don't have a boyfriend?

FRANNIE: Look at it, it can't be more than two days old. Isn't it lovely? Do you know how to tell if the moon is waxing or waning?

HARLON: No.

FRANNIE: If the crescent is this way (*She describes the right half of the circumference of a circle.*) it's waxing; filling out this way. If the crescent is this way (*The left half of the circumference of a circle.*) it's waning. I can always tell what the moon is doing by how I feel. My favorite time to write is just before a full moon, I can stay up two nights in a row writing. Sometimes I can write on a waning moon, but my writing has a very different quality. Very spare.

HARLON: I never met anyone like you.

FRANNIE: Where's the ice? (*He hands her the ice in soda cup in bag.*) Napkins? (*Wraps ice in napkin, gives it to him. He puts it up to his ear.*)

HARLON: You smell good.

FRANNIE: I smell like manure. And mint. There's mint around here, too. You excited?

HARLON: Huh?

FRANNIE: Nervous?

HARLON: . . . yeah.

FRANNIE: (*Looking at the sky.*) Look at all those stars. Did you know that every atom in your body comes from a star? You have atoms in you, stardust atoms, that have memories you aren't even aware of; memories of events that happened in outer space.

HARLON: You sure you can do this?

FRANNIE: Do what?

HARLON: Pierce my ear.

FRANNIE: Sure. Matches? (*He hands her matches. She lights a match to sterilize a needle.*) You know how when people almost die, they see light at the end of a tunnel? They're just remembering their own light, from when they were a star. (*She holds up the match and blows it out.*)

HARLON: Would you care for a Certs?

FRANNIE: (*Still sterilizing the needle.*) No thanks. How's that ice doing?

HARLON: Cold. So. You don't have a boyfriend.

FRANNIE: (*Touching his ear lobe.*) Can you feel this?

HARLON: Do it again. Yeah. I can feel it.

FRANNIE: We'll wait.

HARLON: Can I kiss you?

FRANNIE: No. (*Looking at the sky.*) Last month I watched the Pleiades passing through a day old crescent moon. It was the most lovely romantic thing I've ever seen.

HARLON: You think that's romantic?

FRANNIE: Yes, I do.

HARLON: You think that's romantic?

FRANNIE: Yeah. What do you think is romantic?

HARLON: Kissing.

FRANNIE: Shh!

HARLON: What?

FRANNIE: I thought I heard her moving, inside.

HARLON: She's gonna be your step-mother?

FRANNIE: That's the plan.

HARLON: Do you like her?

FRANNIE: She's okay. She's too paranoid. And wimpy, with my dad. Look!

HARLON: What?

FRANNIE: A shooting star. Oh my God. Oh God, look it's still going, Jesus, it's still going, it's still going, it's still going, still . . . oh. Wasn't that great?

HARLON: Yeah.

FRANNIE: I love shooting stars.

HARLON: I like them too. I don't think I like them as much as you do. (*Pause.*)

FRANNIE: I love summer nights. Soft warm, summer nights, just a little breeze. Crickets, cicadas. The smells -mint, manure, the linden tree, I even love the smells in the garage, the oil, the grease. It's heavenly. Celestial.
(*Pause.*)
You looked really good out there, in center field.

HARLON: Thanks.

FRANNIE: You made some really nice catches.

HARLON: Thanks.

FRANNIE: There was one I was sure you were going to miss, but you got it.

HARLON: Thanks.

FRANNIE: Can you feel this? (*Touches earlobe.*)

HARLON: Do it again. Do it again. Do it again. I don't think so. Do it one more time. No.

FRANNIE: Good. Ready?

HARLON: Uh . . .

FRANNIE: I've got the cork. (*Getting cork out of her pocket. She moves around in from of him, straddling his right leg, her right knee up over his groin. They could be under the top sleeping bag or not. She holds the cork up behind his right earlobe.*) Okay. Let's fly this baby.

HARLON: You can leave your knee there.

FRANNIE: Here we go. You relaxed?

HARLON: You can leave your knee there.

FRANNIE: All right. I may not get all the way through in one go. But don't worry.

HARLON: 'kay.

FRANNIE: Here we go.

(*Pause as she prepares.*)
You're kind of moving around.

HARLON: 'kay.

FRANNIE: I have to get the right angle. I don't want the front hole to be higher than the back hole.

HARLON: 'kay.

FRANNIE: (*Pausing.*) This is harder than I thought it was going to be.

HARLON: (*Beginning to approach orgasm.*) Yeah?

FRANNIE: I'm not sure I can do this.

HARLON: Really?

FRANNIE: I'm afraid I'll hurt you.

HARLON: You won't hurt me.

FRANNIE: You're breathing awful hard. Try not to move around so much. Are you okay?

HARLON: Yeah.

FRANNIE: Okay. Here goes. (*She jabs it.*) Did you feel that?

HARLON: I . . . heard . . . it.

FRANNIE: It's not all the way through. You can't feel it? Can you feel it?

HARLON: Uh . . .

FRANNIE: Try to hold still.

HARLON: 'kay.

FRANNIE: There. You've got a hole in your ear.

HARLON: (*Climaxing.*) Ohh.

FRANNIE: Can you hand me that napkin?
(*He hands her the napkin that had ice in it. She puts napkin on his earlobe, gets him to hold it. She gets off.*)
Did it hurt?

HARLON: No.

FRANNIE: It'll probably hurt a little when it thaws. You okay?

HARLON: Yeah.

FRANNIE: Sure? So. Now you've got a pierced ear. How's it feel?

HARLON: Good.

FRANNIE: You okay?

HARLON: Yup.

FRANNIE: You want the diamond stud or the little gold ball?

HARLON: The diamond.

FRANNIE: Good choice. (*Drops it.*) Oops, in the manure. Lee would have a heart attack over this whole procedure. Little spit. (*Putting it in.*) There. Listen to this little bit of carbon closely, you'll hear tales from the dusty nebulas of space.

HARLON: No.

FRANNIE: No?

HARLON: When I listen to this diamond that I'll hear all the time 'cause it's in my ear, I'll hear your voice, Frannie. That's all. Your voice. And that's all I'll wanna hear.

(*Pause.*)

FRANNIE: Harlon?

HARLON: Yeah?

FRANNIE: You can kiss me if you want to.

HARLON: I do.

FRANNIE: I have to tell you though.

HARLON: What?

FRANNIE: I'm not very clear about it. The mechanics.

HARLON: Huh?

FRANNIE: Should I hold my breath?

HARLON: You never did it before?

FRANNIE: No.

HARLON: You never did it before? You?

FRANNIE: Harlon, just tell me. What should I do?

HARLON: What should you do? Simple. Just . . .

(*He leans toward her slowly as lights fade.*)

THE WHITE ROSE
by Lillian Garrett-Groag

Dramatic / 1 Man, 1 Woman
Sophie: an idealistic young woman opposed to the Nazi
regime and the war, 21
Mohr: head of the Munich Gestapo, 50s

The Setting: Gestapo Headquarters, Munich, 1943

Sophie and her friends have been arrested by the Gestapo for
distributing anti-Nazi pamphlets. In one of many interrogations,
Sophie reveals her passion for life and love of Germany to the
dour Mohr.

O   O   O

MOHR: Several of your connections with other universities have
been arrested.
SOPHIE: *Connections*? I have school friends. We're not political.
MOHR: We're at war. That statement is not acceptable.
SOPHIE: (*Fighting sleep and fear.*) I don't believe in war.
MOHR: (*Quickly closing the door.*) And that statement can put
you in prison for life.
SOPHIE: Should I lie to you?
MOHR: You've been lying to me for two days.
SOPHIE: I don't know what you mean.
MOHR: What exactly is your relationship to Christoph Probst,
Alexander Schmorell, and Wilhelm Graf?
SOPHIE: We study together, we have parties . . .
MOHR: *Printing* parties?
SOPHIE: I don't know what you mean.
MOHR: Do you understand what an accusation of high treason
means? (*Silence.*) What is your relationship to Professor
Huber?
SOPHIE: Huber?
MOHR: Kurt Huber, yes.
SOPHIE: Oh. I took his course. Introduction to philosophy.
MOHR: Did your brother take his course too?

SOPHIE: He . . . may have.

MOHR: You took his course together, very recently.

SOPHIE: I'd forgotten

MOHR: As a matter of fact, all of you have taken that course at one time or another.

SOPHIE: (*Shrugging.*) He's good.

MOHR: But a few moments ago you had trouble remembering his name.

SOPHIE: I don't know what you mean.

MOHR: That seems to be your favorite statement.

SOPHIE: I'm sorry.

MOHR: (*Picking up the leaflets.*) Just how good a teacher is he? Is he the one who fed you all this *cant*?

SOPHIE: I don't . . . what?

MOHR: What is his particular attraction? Why does he have so many students?

SOPHIE: (*Pause.*) He is an extremely patriotic man. These are hard times. He is adamant about – the preservation of German honor.

MOHR: What's his opinion on the Führer?

SOPHIE: (*Very politely.*) He never mentions the Führer in connection to German honor. (*Beat.*) It's an introductory course, you know . . . the Greeks and all that . . . Plato, Socrates, –

MOHR: What about the seventeenth century?

SOPHIE: Some.

MOHR: Spinoza, for instance?

SOPHIE: Spinoza?

MOHR: Spinoza: the Jew.

SOPHIE: Oh, yes. Professor Huber told us we are not to read him.

MOHR: It seems he spent the better part of a week telling you not to read him. *And* Sigmund Freud!

SOPHIE: (*Impenetrable.*) He was explaining how dangerous they are.

(*Beat.*)

MOHR: We know that Professor Huber has – *had*, little soirées, to which his "favorite" pupils were invited and where certain topics were discussed.

SOPHIE: I've never heard of them.

MOHR: I suppose your brother and his friends haven't either?

SOPHIE: We don't go to a lot of parties.

MOHR: But you said you did.

SOPHIE: What?

MOHR: You said you had "parties" together, just a moment ago.

SOPHIE: I . . . what?

MOHR: With your friends. You said you had parties with your friends.

SOPHIE: Oh . . . But not with –

MOHR: Not with the "Professor." I see.

SOPHIE: No.

MOHR: Not even to discuss the "preservation of German honor," whatever that may mean?

SOPHIE: You don't know what it means?

MOHR: It depends on whose terms.

SOPHIE: Honor has no terms. It's the one thing in life that's absolute.

MOHR: Then surely you can explain to me what it is.

SOPHIE: I wouldn't presume to explain to a government official what German honor is . . . or should be.

MOHR: I wouldn't find it presumptuous. I'd find it interesting. Please.

SOPHIE: I don't know the difference between personal honor and national honor. Do you? (*Pause.*)

MOHR: (*Abruptly.*) What about boys, Sophie. Aren't you in love? (*Sophie starts involuntarily.*) Are you in love, Sophie? (*She looks at him.*) What about your parents? Are you fond of them?

SOPHIE: *Fond*? I wouldn't say "fond." "Fond" is a sentimental notion.

MOHR: Think very carefully. Could you not have been influenced by the wrong set of people . . . let us say, a subversive element in our universities, and misled into doing something the implications of which you did not understand? Students, especially young women, are often impressionable, easily confused. This "professor" of yours could turn out to be the only one responsible –

SOPHIE: I don't understand. But, as you say, I'm a girl, and girls are easily confused.

MOHR: Damn it! Don't try to turn the tables on me, Sophie, I'm an old hand at this!

SOPHIE: I don't think so.

MOHR: What?!

SOPHIE: I think you're rather new at this. And you don't like it.

MOHR: (*Exploding.*) What in hell – Do you not want to live?

SOPHIE: Passionately!

MOHR: Passion is for the Opera, Sophie, not for everyday life.

SOPHIE: Too bad for everyday life. (*Pause.*)

MOHR: Look, it's time you went back to your . . .

SOPHIE: Cell? That word doesn't come easily to you. (*Gently.*) You must be in the wrong business.

MOHR: (*Snapping.*) Serving Germany is not a business. It's a privilege.

SOPHIE: You love Germany?

MOHR: What? Certainly, I –

SOPHIE: Because I love Germany . . . passionately. (*Pause.*)

MOHR: Bauer! (*Bauer enters.*) Get me Mahler right away.

[**BAUER:** Yes, sir. (*Bauer exits.*)]

MOHR: (*To Sophie.*) I'll be calling you again.

SOPHIE: I expect you will.

MOHR: (*Looking through his papers.*) Good day.

SOPHIE: I wish it were.

THE YEARS
by Cindy Lou Johnson

Dramatic / 1 Man, 1 Woman
Jeffrey and Eloise: a couple whose marriage is on the verge
of collapse, 30s

The Setting: here and now

On the day of her sister's wedding, Eloise confronts Jeffrey with
her suspicion that he is seeing someone else.

○   ○   ○

JEFFREY: Hi.

ELOISE: (*Turning, startled.*) Oh Jeffrey! You're back! Everything's
gone wrong. Could you hand me the rest of that rope down
there.

JEFFREY: Here you go.

ELOISE: Thanks.

JEFFREY: What's gone wrong?

ELOISE: There's a war or something and Aunt Lee and Uncle Pete
are having a bit of a time getting out of Italy.

JEFFREY: There's no war in Italy.

ELOISE: I don't know then. A typhoon.

JEFFREY: A *typhoon*! In Italy?

ELOISE: I don't know. Something's happened that's making it
impossible to fly. And on top of it, Andrea's gone to work –

JEFFREY: She's at work?

ELOISE: Yes so –
(*Interrupting herself.*)
Could you lift those a little higher?
(*He does.*)
Thanks. How was Arizona?

JEFFREY: It was alright. I rented a little red convertible.

ELOISE: What kind?

JEFFREY: Mustang. I drove around like a son of a bitch.

ELOISE: That sounds nice.

JEFFREY: It was hot out there.

ELOISE: It was?

JEFFREY: Yeah. Up in the nineties. But business went well. Crazy, but well.

ELOISE: (*Glances at him.*) You didn't get burned.

JEFFREY: What?

ELOISE: I mean if it was in the nineties. You didn't get burned.

JEFFREY: I stayed out of the sun.

ELOISE: I thought you were in a convertible.

JEFFREY: Yeah, but I always wore a hat.

ELOISE: Which hat?

JEFFREY: What do you mean?

ELOISE: Which hat did you always wear?

JEFFREY: A baseball cap. My Mets one.

ELOISE: Oh.
   (*She pauses.*)
   Your Mets one?

JEFFREY: Yeah. That's a strange question.

ELOISE: (*She is leaning back to tack in the roses and almost falls.*) Oh.

JEFFREY: Watch it!

ELOISE: I'm ok.

JEFFREY: You just about took a bad fall.

ELOISE: I just lost my balance.

JEFFREY: You ok?

ELOISE: Yeah. Fine.

JEFFREY: Well, I haven't even gone home yet. I just came straight here to say hello. I guess I should go home and get organized.

ELOISE: Get organized?

JEFFREY: Get a shower?

ELOISE: (*Distracted.*) Oh. Yes. I guess so.

JEFFREY: Are we eating a meal before this thing or what?

ELOISE: I don't . . . I don't . . .

JEFFREY: I don't get this getting married at midnight. Don't you think everyone will be awfully sleepy?

ELOISE: We'll make coffee.

JEFFREY: Yeah. Like a bucket. Alright. I'll be back soon.

ELOISE: Jeff.

JEFFREY: Yes?

ELOISE: It's just –
   (*He turns back around.*)

I think your Mets hat is on the hook in the foyer.

JEFFREY: It is?

ELOISE: Yes. You'll see it as soon as you walk in.

JEFFREY: Oh. Well . . . it was some other hat then. I don't know. I'll be back in about an hour or so. (*He starts to leave.*)

ELOISE: It's just all your hats are hanging there.

JEFFREY: Hanging where?

ELOISE: On the hook in the foyer.

JEFFREY: (*Laughing.*) No. Not all of them were hanging there, because one hat was missing because I had it on my head. (*Pauses.*) I think this wedding is making everybody mentally disturbed.

ELOISE: Well, yes . . . I have been a little disturbed, because I had to call you on Saturday. I was looking for your tuxedo, to get it pressed for you, but I couldn't find the cummerbund, so I called you at your hotel, in Tucson, and . . . well, it was closed.

JEFFREY: What?

ELOISE: For renovations. It re-opens in July.

JEFFREY: Oh yeah. I'm sorry.

ELOISE: Sorry?

JEFFREY: I forgot to call and tell you. I went to a different hotel. I was never there anyway. I told you before I left you'd never be able to reach me. There were just meetings around the clock. Did you find my cummerbund?

ELOISE: Yes, I finally –

JEFFREY: I think it was hanging in the closet. Seems like I remember it wrapped around some hook in the closet –

ELOISE: It was in a drawer.

JEFFREY: Oh.

ELOISE: Yes, I assumed it was some kind of situation with the hotel where you –

JEFFREY: Yeah, the whole week was nuts –

ELOISE: It's just – (*She stops.*)

JEFFREY: What?

ELOISE: Well it's just –

JEFFREY: What *is* it?

ELOISE: It's just I don't believe you.

JEFFREY: You don't believe me?

ELOISE: (*Quietly.*) No.

JEFFREY: You just don't *believe* me?

ELOISE: No. I thought I would. I thought you'd say something and it would all make sense, but –

JEFFREY: Fine.

ELOISE: I don't know. I just don't –

JEFFREY: Look, your sister's wedding is in a few hours. I don't think we should –

ELOISE: Just tell me I'm wrong. I don't know why I feel this way. We've kind of lost our way or –

JEFFREY: I really don't want to get into some whole –

ELOISE: If you just tell me I'm wrong then –

JEFFREY: I don't think I should have to –

ELOISE: You don't have to do anything. Just tell me all this stuff has been getting to me and –

JEFFREY: I'm *not* going to get into some whole –

ELOISE: Jeffrey, I'm losing my mind.

JEFFREY: (*After a moment.*) Alright. What do you want to know?

ELOISE: Where you were for the past two days.

JEFFREY: In Colorado.

ELOISE: In Colorado?

(*Jeffrey is silent.*)

With someone?

(*Jeffrey looks away. She suddenly lifts a small ashtray and throws it at him. He ducks. It misses and crashes to the floor.*)

JEFFREY: Jesus!

ELOISE: (*Fairly stunned at what she's done.*) Oh my God!

JEFFREY: (*Collecting himself.*) Alright. Alright . . .

ELOISE: (*Still very quietly.*) You can't ever see her again or talk to her or even –

JEFFREY: I was going to tell you. I just thought – maybe after the wedding.

ELOISE: There's nothing to tell. There's nothing to discuss. I don't want to – Just say you won't ever –

JEFFREY: I can't say that.

ELOISE: What?

JEFFREY: Because I actually will see her.

ELOISE: What?

JEFFREY: I can't lie anymore. I can't stand it.

ELOISE: I don't want you to lie.

JEFFREY: It's Kathleen, Eloise. I'm in love with her.

ELOISE: Kathleen.

JEFFREY: I am. I have been. It's always seemed like the wrong time to deal with it. First your mother dying, and . . .

ELOISE: It's been since *then*?

JEFFREY: But when is the right time? She's losing her mind. I'm losing my mind and now you're –

ELOISE: *She's* losing *her* mind! Oh my God!

JEFFREY: I'm in love with her. I can't help it. It's how I feel. I want to marry her.

ELOISE: What?

JEFFREY: I've . . . We . . . have to part because –

ELOISE: Stop talking.

JEFFREY: We married too young, It's no good –

ELOISE: Stop talking!

JEFFREY: Our lives don't make any sense.

ELOISE: My life makes sense.

JEFFREY: No. It doesn't. It's based on a lie.

ELOISE: Stop talking!

JEFFREY: This is how I feel. I didn't choose it. It's just the truth. I don't want to hurt you.

ELOISE: You don't want to *hurt* me?

JEFFREY: It's not my intention but what can I do?

ELOISE: What can you *do*?

JEFFREY: Eloise, Please try to understand. I –

ELOISE: STOP TALKING!

JEFFREY: I'm going to go.

ELOISE: My sister's getting married.

JEFFREY: Just say – just say I had to go back to Arizona. Say I never got in. Say there was a typhoon!

ELOISE: It's my *sister's* wedding!

JEFFREY: What am I supposed to do? Stand beside you and hold your hand and look – devoted – when we both know –

ELOISE: It's one day. It's my sister's wedding.

JEFFREY: It would be a complete sham.

ELOISE: Jeff please. We've got to talk. We've got to –

JEFFREY: I'm going. (*He moves to the door.*)

ELOISE: Don't leave!

(*She runs up and grabs him. He takes her hands, removes them gently, and exits.*)

Oh my God. Oh my God.

Scenes
For Women

CRUISING CLOSE TO CRAZY
by Laura Cunningham

Serio-Comic / 2 Women
   Carolee and Honey: two country western stars preparing for
      a show, 30-40

The Setting: the bedroom of a country western tour bus, the
present

Carolee is visited in her tour bus by Honey, who finds her friend
in a blue funk. Honey, a rip-snortin' gal who won't take "no"
for an answer, bullies Carolee out of bed and into costume.

CAROLEE: (*Muttering, almost incoherent.*) My mouth's so dry, I
   can't talk . . . Nine times in the hospital . . . I'm dying tonight
   . . . I seen it happen already . . . I was lying in a wine-color
   coffin, in a wine-color room . . . and everybody was walking
   around whispering . . . And he done me dead the way he
   done me alive . . . He don't even show, don't you know: He
   done me dead, like he done me alive . . .
   (*New voice to Honey.*)
   You believe in precognition?
HONEY: I ought to. I knowed when I was in trouble.
CAROLEE: Things happen in your head before they happen to
   you for real?
HONEY: All the time. This song I wrote: I heard it before. Maybe
   in another life.
   (*She hums a tune: a wistful ballad.*)
CAROLEE: (*Picking up the melody.*) "It would still be you . . . If I
   knew a thousand men, in the end, it would still be you . . . If I
   lived and loved and married again, in the end . . . it would still
   be you . . ."
   (*New tone, more dazed than irritated.*)
   Hey, that's my song.
HONEY: "It Would Still Be You" . . . is yours?
CAROLEE: . . . That was my last single!

HONEY: Then how'd it get inside my head?

CAROLEE: (*Oddly not angered but warmed by the plagiarism.*) Well, maybe it was unconscious. You n' me . . . we're like sisters. We look and sound just like.

(*They don't. To audience.*)

Now she's here, she ain't so bad . . .

(*Honey unfurls a paper towel, reads her own handwritten lyric, pencilled onto the improvised scroll.*)

HONEY: "If you were worse than you are . . . If you walked harder across my heart . . . If we were always apart . . . *It would still be you* . . ."

CAROLEE: Well, that's a little different but in a way it's the same. (*She pats Honey.*)

It's alright: I got the copyright. Now just don't tell me – "I Call My Pain by Your Name . . ." is yours, too.

HONEY: No, it's yours.

(*Sweet smile.*)

But you know my version gone gold.

CAROLEE: (*In recognition.*) "Hurt Me."

HONEY: We both made out on that one. You should have stuck with me. We was doing alright. You shouldn't have mixed it up with Jesse Dark . . . It were him, weren't it?

(*Carolee ignores the question, takes the Tabasco-honey sauce, drains it.*)

CAROLEE: (*Distracted, muttering to herself.*) Don't hurt, don't hurt a bit.

HONEY: I told you not to work with him.

(*She uses a new tone as she resumes her own favorite theme: men.*)

Men. Crazy old men. All they know is they got a long thing and you got a hole to put it in. Crazy old men.

(*New insistent tone to Carolee.*)

Admit it. Admit it. Some nights, don't you just want to bite it off?

CAROLEE: I'm not a hater. Maybe it's a man's nature to . . .

HONEY: He'd screw a snake if you held its head down. Pussy's pussy, even if it's on a cow.

CAROLEE: (*Changing the subject.*) How's Max?

HONEY: He's home. He's fine.

(*Automatically asking after Carolee's husband.*)

How's the Duker?

CAROLEE: I ain't seen him in a year.

HONEY: That's good.

CAROLEE: He's raising beef cattle. He sells them . . . I don't want him killing on my farm. I don't *do* my cattle that way. Even if I ain't there to see it: They go.

HONEY: Max is in business for himself: Septic.

CAROLEE: That's good.

HONEY: Well, I go home sometimes. Me and Max, we're not party people: We need time to be human beings. Have a barbeque. Do normal things.
(*Defending her marriage.*)
We love each other; after ten years, we can just love and pet for two hours before we get started. That's how I like it. If a man ain't tender, I kick him in the balls.

CAROLEE: Does it work?

HONEY: Well if it don't, I don't have to worry about it, do I? You don't see me lying and crying in my bus, do you? You going to let Jesse Dark *do* you like this? Don't you think you should get up there, just to show him . . . show everybody . . . You don't care! You're bigger and better than he ever was!

CAROLEE: I can't! I can't get up there with him! You don't know how it was . . . You ain't been with him . . .
(*Caught short by a new doubt.*)
. . . Have you?

HONEY: I don't know if I have or I haven't. I forget.
(*Smile.*) There been a few.

CAROLEE: If you forgot him, you never knew him.

HONEY: Well, you don't have to eat an apple to know it's gone bad. I took a look. Sure. He's something. And he knows it. To me, he has a dirty look.

CAROLEE: (*An involuntary defense.*) He's clean! He takes a lot of showers, and his hair's always washed.

HONEY: I didn't mean dirty that way. I meant it the other way. He's no dresser, though. I'm sick a seeing him in his tee-shirt and jeans. I swear that tee-shirt has had the same holes in it for five years . . . He had holes in his shirt when he did Loner. And he's only worth how many million dollars.

CAROLEE: He's just different, that's all. He's different from the others. They wear studs – he don't wear studs. They wear rhinestones, he don't wear rhinestones. He likes to be just . . . plain.

HONEY: He could spend three dollars on a new shirt and give us a break. And get himself another pair of jeans.

CAROLEE: Well, I know he's bad, but he looks good in his jeans. They're just so worn and soft . . .

(*She breaks off, realizing she sounds affectionate.*)

HONEY: When they're built, they get away with a lot. His kind. That's the worst. Snake hips. That's what he is. That's how Lucifer appears to woman, you know: Snake hips. You read your Bible, close, you'll see what they're really talking about . . . You see a man grow wide as his hips is narrow, run and hide. That man is the devil and he going to ride you straight to hell . . .

CAROLEE: I know: You're right. He left me for dead.

HONEY: They say he takes two women a night. One after each show. Not two together. One each time.

(*She reflects.*)

He likes his privacy.

CAROLEE: He's a very private person.

HONEY: Considerin' he slept with half the world.

(*New squint at Carolee.*)

It true what they say about him?

CAROLEE: Whut?

HONEY: They say he goes six times without stopping. He that way with you?

(*Carolee refuses to answer.*)

Well, you went on tour with him . . . You done fourteen cities . . . He that way with you?

CAROLEE: (*Shy, but bragging.*) I ain't saying.

HONEY: (*Appraising the situation.*) It was good; that's why it's bad.

CAROLEE: (*Breaking down, a bit.*) I can't come back from it, Honey . . . I just can't . . . He took everything from me when he went.

HONEY: Well, then you just have to get him back.

(*New look.*)

I can tell you how. I know his kind. He may be the Devil, but even the Devil can be tamed. You ride him harder than he rode you: You crack the whip! You don't take nothing from him! You stay on top! He thinks he can't have you – he come running . . . You just got to play it hard to get . . .

(*As she speaks, Honey is excitedly working the hot curlers into a wig. She adjusts Carolee on the bed, so she can "do" her hair. Yanking a comb, then setting the straggled locks on hot rollers.*)

CAROLEE: (*Passively accepting the advice and the hairdressing.*) Well, how can I be hard to get when I been got?

HONEY: It's in your head, how he sees you. You got to turn it around. You don't give an inch.

CAROLEE: I can't.

HONEY: (*A bit cross.*) The one thing I won't tolerate is negativity. You think positive – you be anything, you have anything or anyone you want.

CAROLEE: Well, maybe he did like me a little? He wouldn't a done some of what he done, or said some of what he said, if he didn't like me just a bit? Would he?

(*Losing herself in revery.*)

You ever see a beautiful man go meek – you know – just *before* – go all shy on you and look down at his feet?

HONEY: (*Working the hair curlers, distracted.*) A beautiful man? No. The homely ones go meek all the time. (*With bobby pin in her teeth.*) They ought to be meek.

CAROLEE: Well, it was really something. It was so sweet, it hurt me to see it . . .

(*Gaining strength.*)

Well, he must have liked me *then* . . .

HONEY: Of course he did. Now all you have to do is call his bus and tell him: "Git your arse over here, Shithead. I got something to say. And if I don't say it *before* the show, I'm going to say it *during*, so a couple thousand people can hear it live and millions more on tape . . ." He'll be here before these curlers are cool.

CAROLEE: Well, I got nothing to lose.

(*Thinking.*)

I lost it all in Albuquerque . . .

HONEY: Just don't give him none before the show. You make his old tongue hang out for it. If you give him some, he'll be cracking the old whip again. You make him wait. Wait till after the show.

(*New tone.*)

It's easier on your hair that way, too.

CAROLEE: (*Assenting on the plan.*) Will you do my face?

HONEY: I know just how.

(*Honey slathers on the makeup: outlining Carolee's eyes, smearing on hot pink blusher. Surveying her work.*)

Now you look human. Now watch you don't get this stuff all over your dress. It'll be one fine mess to get off. I use Wisk on mine. It's saved me a thousand dollars. I used to have to throw them out.

(*Honey seizes the violet dress, unzips it, helps Carolee into it. As the dress is lowered over Carolee's exposed emaciated body, Honey gives the other woman her critique.*)

Your boobs is slippin' . . .

CAROLEE: I know. That doctor in Vegas didn't know what he was doing. In another year, I'm going to have one boob down to my belly.

HONEY: I didn't know you had your kids by Caesarean . . .

CAROLEE: Only the first two. I was too young, too small . . . You can hardly have 'em when you're only twelve, you know . . . But I had the other three natural . . . (*Sad.*) My bones spread apart each time . . .

HONEY: Don't think about your kids – they're all growed. It's time for you to think about yourself.

CAROLEE: I know. I didn't know nothing when I married Duker. I thought you was supposed to bleed every time.

HONEY: He weren't tender?

CAROLEE: Tender! I spent my wedding night in the emergency room!

HONEY: Crazy old men. All they know is they got a long thing and you got a hole to put it in . . ..

CAROLEE: Well, I bought him his own town: He can stay in it.

HONEY: I don't know why you just don't divorce him.

CAROLEE: I don't know myself. I guess I thought – Well, they're all assholes. I *know* this asshole.

HONEY: He'd screw a snake, you hold its head down. Pussy's pussy, even when it's on a cow.

CAROLEE: (*Referring to her grooming methods.*) Take it easy! You're pulling my skin!

(*Looking down at herself.*)

Sometimes I think my skin's grown a size large: It just hanging here like last year's costume. Yeah, a size large.

HONEY: Well, at least you're skinny. I can't eat again until 1996. Not real food. And then, no fried.

(*Honey finishes zipping up the costume.*)

Here . . . You're done up. Now call Jesse Dark and get it over with . . .

CAROLEE: I can't!

HONEY: Well, all right, I'll do it.

(*Honey goes to phone by bedside. Into phone.*)

Hey . . . who's this? Well this is Honey. Yeah. I'm on Carolee's bus. Who's this? Breadman! How are you, you old fool! Is the man there? Yeah? Well tell him to get his arse over to Carolee's bus . . . Right now if he knows what's good for him. Great. Love ya!

(*She hangs up, turns beaming to Carolee.*)

See, that weren't so hard, was it?

CAROLEE: You're something. I wish I could be like you.

(*Musing.*)

Casual. Men love you when you're casual.

HONEY: It's not love, it's fascination. Let me comb you out . . . then I'm getting out of here . . .

(*Honey teases Carolee's own hair and wigs into one wild mane. Rather astonishingly, from an aesthetic distance, Carolee looks quite spectacular. Honey studies her work.*)

Well, Annie Oakley weren't nothing! There could be a prettier girl singer than you – I don't know who.

CAROLEE: I love you for this, Honey.

DAVID'S MOTHER
by Bob Randall

Serio-Comic / 2 Women
> Sally: a woman who has sacrificed everything for her
> handicapped son, 40s
> Bea: her sister, 40s

The Setting: an apartment in Manhattan, the present

Sally has struggled for years to keep her son from being institutionalized, and Bea has done her best to be supportive – right down to finding a wealthy man for Sally to marry. Here, years of guilt and frustration explode between the two sisters.

O   O   O

SALLY: (*Turning, in the past now.*) You want me to zap you something?
BEA: When's the last time you cooked?
SALLY: I don't know. What's-his-name was still here.
BEA: His name's Phil.
SALLY: He left five months ago, so I haven't cooked in five months. It's one of the many benefits of not having him around.
BEA: (*Beat, uncomfortable with this.*) He called me last night.
SALLY: Yeah?
BEA: He signed a lease on an apartment in the Village.
SALLY: Good. Every village should have an idiot.
BEA: There's a place there for special ed kids that's supposed to be good. Only you have to live in the district to be eligible.
SALLY: So?
BEA: So, David's father lives in the district!
SALLY: I'm not putting David in any home, Bea.
BEA: It's not a home. It's a school. Besides, Phil said he'd pick him up every Tuesday afternoon and keep him overnight. You know what that means?
SALLY: It means one idiot would take care of another.
BEA: It means you could have a couple of days off. Come on, he's

his father. Let him do some of the work.

SALLY: Forget it.

BEA: For crying-out-loud, why?! You're denying yourself to punish Phil.

SALLY: He walked out on his own kid! David is as much his fault as mine. I'm not going to let him ease his conscience by taking him out for pizza once a week.

BEA: (*Beat.*) "Fault?!" David isn't anyone's fault. One out of ten kids is born impaired. He's one of the one out of ten, that's all.

SALLY: Fine. It's nobody's fault.

BEA: Well, it isn't!

SALLY: (*Bitterly.*) God, that's so nice! It must be wonderful to live in a world that's so nice. No fault accidents, no fault murders . . . It's so damn *nice*.

BEA: Why are you attacking me?

SALLY: Because it's bullshit! They don't have a clue what caused David to be born with scrambled eggs instead of a brain, but *you* know it wasn't me? I wish *I* knew that, Bea, I wish I knew it was the fluoride in the water or the asbestos in the ceiling or the lead in the fucking paint. I wish to Christ I wasn't on the list of suspects for the joint I smoked when I was carrying him or the wine I was so sure couldn't hurt him or the sex in the eighth month or some genetic fuck up in my chromosomes!

BEA: Stop that! You'll drive yourself crazy thinking things like that! Stop that right now!

SALLY: (*Begrudgingly.*) Alright, I stopped.

BEA: It's Ma's fault.

SALLY: What's Ma's fault?

BEA: She always blamed you so now you blame you. Come here, I want to hold you in my arms.

SALLY: Don't be ridiculous.

BEA: (*Crossing to her with open arms.*) Let me hold you.

SALLY: (*Starting to laugh, backing up.*) Get away from me, you moron.

BEA: Let me hold you!

SALLY: Oh, Christ. (*Begrudgingly, Sally permits Bea to embrace and hold her. Beat.*) "The Children's Hour." Shirley MacLaine and Audrey Hepburn.

(*Bea starts to laugh and releases her.*)

BEA: (*Forcing herself to stop laughing.*) You don't always have to make jokes. I know how much you hurt. I know how much you want Phil back.

SALLY: What?! Bea, listen to me carefully. See if you recognize any of these words. I don't want him back. I wouldn't take him back if you presented him to me on a silver platter with an apple up his ass! Am I getting through to you?

BEA: (*Not believing a word.*) Yeah, yeah.

SALLY: Would you please stop being the authority on my feelings?!

BEA: Alright, I'm sorry. I just think somebody besides you should bear some of the burden. What if, God forbid . . .

SALLY: Say it, I won't drop dead because you said it.

BEA: Well?

SALLY: I don't want to talk about it.

BEA: It wouldn't kill him to take David overnight.

SALLY: Sure. Him and his girlfriend. I wouldn't trust that bleached tramp to watch my kid for two minutes.

BEA: He'd be with his father.

SALLY: (*Sarcastically.*) What's second prize?

BEA: How do you know she's bleached? You've seen her!

SALLY: Yeah. I dropped Susan off at his office a couple of months ago. I could tell which one she was.

BEA: How?

SALLY: She didn't look up from her typewriter once. She just sat there, her face red and blotchy and pounded the keys. She's a little fat thing. She wore a high-collared dress to cover her big tits and hardly any makeup. Just a little baby blue eye shadow, like some sweet little virgin. And her hair was dyed a very nice color, if you happen to be a golden hamster. She looked like she should have been carrying a tray of beer steins at an Octoberfest. I had quite a good look at her while we waited for Phil. After five minutes, she started to sweat. I hoped she'd drip into her electric typewriter and set herself on fire, but no luck. She just sat there, hunting and pecking like crazy. She looked like a kid at a piano recital with her mother in the audience with a gun. And then she gave this miniature sneeze, like a bug, and she dabbed at her nose with a ladylike hanky and I said "Bless you" and she said "Thank you" but her eyes never left the typewriter. And I knew it was her. I hoped Phil wouldn't show up for an hour so when he did his girlfriend would be sitting there, her rodent hair matted to the side of her head by sweat, two baby blue rivers pouring down her fat cheeks, her heart pounding like a set of bongos beneath her stretched out dress. But he showed up and I left. But not before I said something to her.

BEA: (*Enjoying this.*) What?

SALLY: Just "Have a nice day." Out of all the things I could have said, to let her know I knew who she was, to make her spit like a pig on a rotisserie, all that came out was "Have a nice day." I ask you, am I a saint or what?

BEA: (*Getting up, crossing to kitchen.*) A saint? You're an idiot. If it were my Stephen, she would have been wearing her typewriter as an I.U.D.

GOODNIGHT DESDEMONA
(GOOD MORNING JULIET)
by Ann-Marie MacDonald

Serio-Comic / 2 Women
Desdemona: the war-like wife of Othello, 20-30
Constance: a mousy assistant professor of Renaissance
Drama, 20-30

The Setting: the home of Othello, Cyprus

Constance is magically transported into the Shakespearean tale of "Othello," and immediately saves Desdemona's life by thwarting Iago. Here, she turns to the Moor's bloodthirsty bride for help.

O   O   O

DESDEMONA: *If I do vow a friendship, I'll perform it
to the last article.*
Othello's honour is my own. If you do find me foul in this,
then let thy sentence fall upon my life;
as I am brave Othello's faithful wife.
(*Desdemona seizes Constance and squeezes her in a soldierly
embrace.*)
CONSTANCE: Thanks.
(*A blast of trumpets.*)
Ah-h!
DESDEMONA: Ah, supper. That have killed a suckling pig in
honour of thee.
CONSTANCE: I'm a vegetarian.
That is – I don't eat . . . flesh. Of any kind.
DESDEMONA: Such abstinence is meet in vestal vows,
therefore in all points do I find thee true.
I'd serve thee, Pedant! Beg of me a boon!
Though it be *full of poise and difficult weight,
and fearful to be granted*, I'll perform it!
CONSTANCE: There is a problem you could help me with.
I'm not sure how to say this.

DESDEMONA: Speak it plain.

CONSTANCE: Alright, I will. I'm from another world –

DESDEMONA: Ay, Academe. And ruled by mighty Queens,
a race of Amazons who brook no men.

CONSTANCE: It's really more like –

DESDEMONA: Nothing if not war-like!
I'd join these ranks of spiked and fighting shes:
to camp upon the deserts vast and sing
our songs of conquest, and a dirge or two
for sisters slain on honour's gory field.

CONSTANCE: If only I could bring you home with me.

DESDEMONA: I'll anywhere with thee, my friend.

CONSTANCE: That's it, you see, I can't return until – That is . . .
my Queens have charged me with a fearful task:
I must find my true identity,
and then discover who the author be.

DESDEMONA: Thou dost not know thyself?

CONSTANCE: Apparently not.

DESDEMONA: Do none in Academe know who thou art?

CONSTANCE: Maybe. They call me Connie to my face,
and something else behind my back.

DESDEMONA: What's that?

CONSTANCE: "The Mouse."

DESDEMONA: "The Mouse?"

CONSTANCE: I saw it carved into a lecture stand.

DESDEMONA: The sculptor dies.

CONSTANCE: Ironic really, since in my world,
women are supposed to be afraid of mice.

DESDEMONA: O fie, that's base! Where be the Amazons?

CONSTANCE: In fact they're few and far between
and often shoved to th' fringe.

DESDEMONA: Let's fly to their beleaguered side.

CONSTANCE: My tasks.

DESDEMONA: The first task is performed already, Con,
thou art an Amazon.

CONSTANCE: I'm not so sure.

DESDEMONA: As to the second task, the Author find.
There be no authors here, but warriors.

CONSTANCE: I'm looking for the Author of it all.
How can I put this? Who made you?

DESDEMONA: God made me.

CONSTANCE: But do you know another name for God?

DESDEMONA: God's secret name?

CONSTANCE: That's it! God's secret name.

DESDEMONA: Seek not to know what God would keep a mystery.

CONSTANCE: Have you known God to be called Shakespeare?

DESDEMONA: Shake Spear? He might be a pagan god of war.

CONSTANCE: This isn't Shakespeare. It must be a source.
Then I was right about the Manuscript!

DESDEMONA: Manuscript?

CONSTANCE: The book that conjured . . . this.
It's written by that secret name of God.
If I could find those foolscap pages –

DESDEMONA: Fool's cap?

CONSTANCE: About yea long, and written in a code;
they fell into the garbage. So did I.

DESDEMONA: This Garbage, be it ocean, lake or sea?

CONSTANCE: . . . A sea then – if you like – Sargasso Sea.

DESDEMONA: I'll call this quest mine own, my constant friend.
Though I should drown in deep Sargasso Sea,
I'll find thine unknown Author and Fool's Cap,
for I do love thee! And when I love thee not,
chaos is come again.
(*A cannon blast. Constance is badly startled. Battle cries within.*)
The infidel!
This volley heralds battle with the Turk.
Let's to the sea wall and enjoy the fray!

CONSTANCE: Oh no, I can't. I can't stand violence.

DESDEMONA: If thou wouldst know thyself an Amazon,
acquire a taste for blood. I'll help thee. Come.
(*She takes Constance's hand and starts to lead her off. Constance pulls back.*)

CONSTANCE: No, please!!! I won't look. I'll be sick. I can't even kill a mosquito!

DESDEMONA: Thou shalt be et alive in Cyprus, Con.
Learn to kill.

CONSTANCE: No!

DESDEMONA: That's a fault! Thy sole deficiency.

An errant woman that would live alone,
no husband there, her honour to defend,
must study to be bloody and betimes.

CONSTANCE: Please promise me you'll follow your advice.

DESDEMONA: So will we both. And we be women; not mice.
Come go with me.

CONSTANCE: Okay, I'll be right there. (*Desdemona exits.*)
They can't use real blood, can they?

THE HOPE ZONE
by Kevin Heelan

Dramatic / 2 Women
>Countess: a woman who has waged a long and successful
>war against alcoholism, 50-60
>Maureen: her alcoholic daughter, 30s

The Setting: Oceanside apartments

Due to her alcohol abuse, Maureen is no longer capable of taking care of her young son. Here, she asks her mother for help.

O   O   O

COUNTESS: . . .whatsa matter? You got a look on ya.

MAUREEN: . . .do I?

COUNTESS: . . . are ya feelin' . . . cause I guess we haven't talked, the phone or anything have we . . .

MAUREEN: . . . no. . .

COUNTESS: . . . for *awhile* gone by I guess huh?. . .

MAUREEN: . . . do you have any room for a little bit? (*Beat.*)

COUNTESS: . . . one of the apartments downstairs the occupant is takin' a few weeks in Baltimore I have . . .

MAUREEN: . . . sure?

COUNTESS: . . . well, how long, are you stayin' long, did ya plan or . . .?

MAUREEN: . . . I dunno. Right at *this* point, no . . .

COUNTESS: . . . ok . . .

MAUREEN: . . . but . . . (*Beat.*)

COUNTESS: . . . cause where is Bud?

MAUREEN: . . . with June?

COUNTESS: . . . in Salisbury then . . .

MAUREEN: . . . he's fine . . .

COUNTESS: . . . why leave him forty minutes away? Why didn't you just bring him on in like you usually do?

MAUREEN: Countess . . .

COUNTESS: What? (*Beat.*) *What?*

MAUREEN: Can you take him?

COUNTESS: Take him how? What means the question?

MAUREEN: . . . well, that's the thing . . .

COUNTESS: . . . take him in what capacity?

MAUREEN: . . . in that I can't probably be a good mother anymore now.

COUNTESS: . . . anymore means . . . ?

MAUREEN: . . . well, I had an incident that occurred.

COUNTESS: . . . kind of incident?

MAUREEN: . . . I left him . . .

COUNTESS: . . . *Bud* this is . . .

MAUREEN: . . . as I was going to the store in a parking lot. Yea. Bud.

COUNTESS: . . . and . . . ?

MAUREEN: . . . I – . . .

COUNTESS: . . . cause he's not dead is he?

MAUREEN: . . . oh, no no no . . .

COUNTESS: . . . he *really* is in – ?

MAUREEN: . . . Salisbury, he's in Salisbury, no no . . .

COUNTESS: . . . ok . . .

MAUREEN: . . . No, no he's fine. He's fine. But I *locked* him in. To be safe . . .

COUNTESS: . . . for the store . . .

MAUREEN: . . . I had a short list . . .

COUNTESS: . . . in a car this was . . .

MAUREEN: . . . in a car . . .

COUNTESS: . . . ok . . .

MAUREEN: . . . but . . . I went to the bar next to where the store was . . .

COUNTESS: . . . what time of day?

MAUREEN: . . . see, that's it.

COUNTESS: . . . was it hot? Was this still New Mexico?

MAUREEN: . . . yes. . . (*Beat.*) For hours. That's the thing.

COUNTESS: . . . you left him for hours in the car.

MAUREEN: . . . that's why I say could you take him . . .

COUNTESS: . . . Jesus H. Christ. IN THE HOT SUN CAR!!!?? ARE YOU OUT OF YOUR MIND??

MAUREEN: . . . I drove all the way to here, and I was going the whole time –

COUNTESS: . . . was the window cracked?

MAUREEN: . . . "Get him away from me as quickly as it could possibly take. Before something else."

COUNTESS: . . . oh Maureen . . .

MAUREEN: . . . I know . . .

COUNTESS: . . . that is foul, foul business this is . . .filthy stuff.

MAUREEN: . . . that's why I came.

COUNTESS: Lemmee take and slow down here. Jesus. Get on that even playin' field. Cause I could punch your face. (*Pause.*)

MAUREEN: The window *was* cracked. (*Pause.*)

COUNTESS: So things have obviously got worse for you. From the last visit.

MAUREEN: . . . sort of . . . how do I look?

COUNTESS: (*Lying.*) Fine.
(*Maureen coughs up blood into a handkerchief.*)

MAUREEN: Cause I have this now . . .
(*Maureen shows her the handkerchief.*)

COUNTESS: How long you want me to take him? (*Silence.*) Cause you don't mean for good. Do you mean for good?

MAUREEN: That's what I thought I would see.

COUNTESS: . . . Jesus . . .

MAUREEN: . . . I know . . .

COUNTESS: . . . Jesus *H* . . .

MAUREEN: . . . it's completely that there is no one else to blame but me.

COUNTESS: (*Thinks.*) You go downstairs, and this is for *just now* . . .

MAUREEN: . . . sure . . .

COUNTESS: . . . this is not a permanent *any*thing.

MAUREEN: . . . gotcha . . .

COUNTESS: . . . to the vacant apartment that I had said . . .

MAUREEN: . . . downstairs . . .

COUNTESS: . . . door's open. They're all clean too, the sheets.

MAUREEN: . . . thank you.

COUNTESS: . . . I didn't wash them for *you*.

MAUREEN: . . . *you* didn't wash them. Newton washed them. (*Beat.*)

COUNTESS: Did you never went to try a meeting or got any treatment or anything? Still?

MAUREEN: No. No way am I doing that stuff that's the way I looked at it all this time.

COUNTESS: . . . cause you are gonna be doin' it now.

MAUREEN: . . . least I'll be with the best.

COUNTESS: . . . is no *best*. (*Beat*.) . . . be ridiculous. Are you hungry?

MAUREEN: . . . no, just, ya know . . . what is life worth anyhow mood. . .

COUNTESS: . . . right now I think you *deserve* that mood . . .

MAUREEN: . . . really?

COUNTESS: . . . yes ma'am . . .

MAUREEN: . . . well who are you?

COUNTESS: . . . mean who am I?

MAUREEN: . . . to talk? Nobody. Nobody at all. (*Beat*.)

COUNTESS: . . . geddownstairs.

HOUSE OF WONDERS
by Kate Aspengren

Serio-Comic / 2 Women
  Holly: a frustrated writer, 30s
  Myrta: Holly's great-aunt, dead for 50 years, 40s

The Setting: a studio apartment, the present

Holly has taken an advance from her publisher to write a book about her great-aunt, Myrta Jane Wonders, who ran a brothel in Alaska. After Holly suffers weeks of writer's block, her friends suggest that they try to contact Myrta in a seance to help give Holly some inspiration. Much to Holly's surprise, their plan works.

O　　　O　　　O

(*Holly is in bed. The lights are off. A tape is playing. It is tinkly New Age music – suggesting that perhaps it is a subliminal message tape.*)

MYRTA: Wake up.

HOLLY: (*Confused.*) What? Who's there?

MYRTA: Wake yourself up, little miss.

HOLLY: (*Now more awake.*) Get out of here! I have a gun. I'll use it.
  (*She turns on a lamp next to the bed. Myrta is standing at the foot of the bed, wiping her face. Holly is holding a water pistol in the shape of a dolphin.*)

MYRTA and HOLLY: Jesus!

HOLLY: You're her.

MYRTA: You got me wet. You shot water in my eye, you little ninny.

HOLLY: You're dead!

MYRTA: Dead. Not waterproof.

HOLLY: How?

MYRTA: You know, for a writer you sure use short little sentences. Must take you whole weeks to write a paragraph.

HOLLY: (*Gets slowly out of bed, trying to gain her composure.*)

I'm Holly, your grand niece.

MYRTA: I *know* who you are.

HOLLY: And you're Myrta Jane Wonders.

MYRTA: I know who I am too.

HOLLY: Oh, wow. Lucid dreaming. I've read about this. God, I hope I don't wake up.

MYRTA: It's no dream, little miss. And how can you stand to have that guy talking to you all the time?

HOLLY: What guy?

MYRTA: (*Pointing to the tape recorder.*) *That* one. With that sicky sweet voice. "You are creative and responsive to the world around you. You are the master of your own destiny." What a load of manure. If I'd been master of my own destiny, I wouldn't have dropped dead at forty.

HOLLY: (*Turning off tape recorder.*) You can hear that? It's supposed to be subliminal.

MYRTA: Well, sub-whatever, it's annoying the hell out of me. Now, you and your hare-brained friends brought me here. What do you want?

HOLLY: Brought you . . . ?

MYRTA: With that damnable board. That Ouija thing. Do you know what it's like when someone uses one of those – no, of course you don't – you're still above ground.

Let me tell you what it's like.

You're there, tryin' to live your afterlife – you know, one day at a time – and all of a sudden there's this annoyin' sound. Kinda like the buzz of a real tiny mosquito. Only you don't see anything to swat. It gets louder and louder and then you can hear that it's no mosquito at all. It's voices. Tinny-soundin' little voices in the back of your brain. Callin' you. (*She imitates Rachel.*) "Myrta Jane, can you hear us? Are you with us?"

HOLLY: (*Incredulous.*) You heard us?

MYRTA: Hell yes, I heard you.

HOLLY: I'm sorry. I mean, I never meant to disturb you. I never thought those things really worked.

MYRTA: You would be surprised at the stuff that's real, missy. Anyway, it worked didn't it? You got answers from it.

HOLLY: Well, sure, you get answers. I just always assumed it was one of the people with the pointer, pushing it around. I never figured it was the real person.

MYRTA: Usually it's not.

HOLLY: What?

MYRTA: Usually it's not the real person.

HOLLY: But a minute ago you said it was.

MYRTA: I said the thing worked and you got answers. I didn't say they were from a real person.

HOLLY: I think I'm really confused.

MYRTA: There are people who answer those things for other folks. Sometimes they know the answers and give the true one, sometimes they don't and they have a little fun with it. It's like having a secretary. You don't want to answer the phone, or you're busy or something. Somebody else does it for you.

HOLLY: (*Thinking a moment.*) Okay. When I was in the eighth grade, we had a slumber party at my friend Tootie's house. We tried to call that Mary Jo woman who drowned in Ted Kennedy's car. (*Tries to remember name.*) Mary Jo Kopechne! Anyway, the pointer went crazy that night. Spelled out all kinds of weird stuff and scared us all to death. Sherry Cherry wet the bed – peed right through her sleeping bag and left a big wet spot on Tootie's carpet.

Were we talking to Mary Jo?

MYRTA: (*Shaking her head.*) No, probably not. She's a real popular one. No, there's a guy named Harold – Harold Bookey. Now he usually takes a lot of her calls.

HOLLY: We were talking to a person named Harold?

MYRTA: Yeah, but you never knew and you had a great time. Probably teased that Cherry kid for years about peeing the bed.

(*Holly laughs in agreement.*)

Harold is quite the guy. Died in '57 in Beatrice, Nebraska. Stuck his head out the bedroom window during a tornado to see what all the ruckus was about and – zip! Twister sucked his head right off.

He's a real funny guy. Real popular. Head sits a little crooked though.

Tell me, did the board talk about bugs?

HOLLY: Bugs?

MYRTA: You know, bugs. Insects. Crawly things. Did it mention them at all?

HOLLY: Well, yeah. I do remember that. It kept repeating tarantula, tarantula, over and over. I just thought it was just somebody trying to scare Sherry Cherry. She had a thing about spiders.

MYRTA: (*Laughing.*) Yeah, that's Harold. He used to work for one of those bug companies. The ones that spray your house with nasty stuff? Every time Harold talks through the board he mentions bugs. Caterpillars or cockroaches or something. It's his trademark, I guess you could say. Everybody has one. Like a signature.

(*Pause.*)

HOLLY: I am talking to a ghost about the pest control man.

MYRTA: Don't call me a ghost, missy. Ghosts were invented by the living to scare themselves into stayin' alive. There's no such thing as a ghost.

HOLLY: What's right then? Spirit?

MYRTA: Spirits got no body. Don't you see a body here?

HOLLY: Yes, I do. Angel?

MYRTA: Please.

HOLLY: Enlighten me then. What is the acceptable term for a dead person with whom you're having a conversation?

MYRTA: Dead isn't good enough for you?

HOLLY: It just seems so – I don't know – so final.

MYRTA: Alive is what's final. Not dead.

HOLLY: This is too weird. I am not having this conversation.

MYRTA: I told you before, this is no dream. Now if I were you, I'd take advantage of it. You got me here. What do you want?

HOLLY: (*Sighs.*) Okay, I might as well go along with it. I'm in a kind of a bind.

MYRTA: Go on.

HOLLY: I'm supposed to have a book written – about you – and I don't have much done so far.

MYRTA: Why about *me*?

HOLLY: It's for a series call Famous Foremothers. They've asked some women writers to write about an interesting female relative. I wrote a little synopsis – about my great aunt who was a businesswoman in Alaska. They snapped it up. Gave me a nice cash advance. Which I spent a long time ago.
Now I'm stuck with writing the damn thing.

MYRTA: (*Looking at bookshelf.*) *You* wrote all of those?

HOLLY: Yes, I did.

MYRTA: So who is this Sue McGrew?

HOLLY: She's a nurse. And an amateur detective. She works at different places, solves mysteries, has romances. I made her up.

MYRTA: (*Reading titles.*) Sue McGrew – Resort Nurse, Sue McGrew – Olympic Nurse. Backstage Nurse, Farm Nurse, Space Shuttle Nurse.

This McGrew gal has trouble holding a job, doesn't she?

HOLLY: (*Laughing.*) No one seems to notice.

MYRTA: Do people read these?

HOLLY: Yeah. Lots of people. Mostly teen-aged girls. They buy a lot of them.

MYRTA: You make money doing this?

HOLLY: Yeah, pretty good money. And then sometimes people pay me to come give speeches.

MYRTA: Did you used to be a nurse or something?

HOLLY: No. I wanted to be one. From the time I was little. Pictured myself in some emergency room, saving lives, being a hero. But I found out that you can't be a hero unless you pass chemistry. So I started writing about them. I guess I wanted Sue McGrew to prove that I would have been a great nurse.

MYRTA: Did it work?

HOLLY: Yeah, I think it did. Some nurses' group made Sue McGrew their nurse of the year. And four nursing schools have made me an honorary RN just because they like the way I've portrayed their profession.

MYRTA: Bet they'd be surprised to know it all happened because you were mad that you couldn't get into their school. Now here they are givin' you awards.

HOLLY: (*Laughs.*) One of them gave me that fifty-pound bronze nurse's cap over there. It's got my name engraved on it and everything. (*Holly points to the cap on the top bookshelf.*)

MYRTA: Well, now, it's no wonder Ruthie was so proud of you.

HOLLY: Ruthie? Grandma? You mean Grandma? Have you seen her?

MYRTA: 'Course I have. She's my sister. I was the one who went to get her when she died.

HOLLY: They send somebody to get you? What about that white light thing? I thought you saw a white light, then you saw all your friends and relatives lined up, sort of beckoning you or helping you to the other side or something.

(*Myrta tries to conceal a smile.*)

What? Tell me?

MYRTA: There is no white light.

HOLLY: Of course there is. Everybody knows that. All the people who die and get brought back say so. I saw a whole show on the Discovery channel about it.

MYRTA: I hate to disillusion you, little sister, but since you're family, I'll let you in on a secret. There is no white light. We only do that with the ones we know are going back. They say it happened so everybody keeps waiting for that white light that isn't coming. It's kind of a joke.

HOLLY: A joke? That's really cruel.

MYRTA: Excuse us all to pieces, missy, but we have to do something for amusement. Do you have any idea how long an eternity is?

HOLLY: (*Sits at the table, shaking her head.*) This is the strangest night of my life. What really happens if there's no white light?

MYRTA: Promise not to tell?

HOLLY: Of course I promise. Who'd believe me?

MYRTA: Okay, okay. I'll tell you. What happens is they send a messenger. Someone you know and trust. That person shows up and says, "Time's up. The party's over. All aboard for Cloud City." Or words to that effect. Then there's this big road, like a huge train with fifty boxcars is rollin' right by you. And then you're dead. Simple as that.

ISABELLA DREAMS THE NEW WORLD
by Lenora Champagne

Serio-Comic / 2 Women
  Iberia: a woman of Spanish-Acadian descent, 30s
  Irma: her young daughter

The Setting: Louisiana, the present

Here, mother and daughter share a rainy afternoon while waiting for Irma's father to come home.

O   O   O

IRMA: I saw a rainbow!

IBERIA: That means you'll find gold someday.

IRMA: Soon?

IBERIA: Not today.

IRMA: I'm all wet.

IBERIA: Go put on some dry clothes.

IRMA: I'm hungry.

IBERIA: Hurry and change and you can have some fruit while I finish the biscuits.
That child has too much energy. That's not the Cajun side – it must be the Nunez blood.
(*Irma returns*.)
Look at those shoelaces flapping!

IRMA: Iberia knows it's time for me to learn to tie them myself, but she can't accept that someday I'll no longer need her. These loose shoelaces are a kind of insurance that I won't get very far if I try to walk away. I want a banana.

IBERIA: There are no bananas. Have a plum.

IRMA: A plum isn't enough. Give me all of them.
(*Iberia hands her the fruit bowl. Irma takes the plums and crawls under the table*.)

IBERIA: She likes to sit under there while I work overhead. She told me once that the house is mine, but under the table is hers. I allow her this territory, since it's close by and not a space I can use.

(Iberia rolls out the biscuit dough. She cuts holes in the dough with a glass cutter. Irma eats a plum under the table. The juice runs down her chin.)

For a while we work without speaking, the silence broken only by the smacking of plums, the clinking of knives cutting in the Crisco, the clump of the drinking glass clapped on the dough to stamp out the biscuit rounds. Then Irma pipes up.

IRMA: What is a tidal wave?

IBERIA: A tidal wave is water plus wind. No, that's essence of hurricane.

IRMA: How is a hurricane like sugar cane?

IBERIA: No, sweetness; it beats you down.

Irma laughed at the joke. Her little foot stuck out from the table as she threw herself onto the floor.

IRMA: Tell me about the children tied to the tree.

IBERIA: Didn't you hear, only the children lashed to the top branches of the oak tree survived; the father was washed away; the mother smothered in mud. A man with a boat floated by and heard their cries. He took his knife and cut them out of the tree branches looking like a bush in that deep water. His wife had to raise them. Ha. She never forgave. She had her hands full of enough children. She made them slave and when they were ungrateful she beat them to remind them how lucky they were. All they remember all their lives is lashes. Lashed to the tree, lashed by her, cut to the quick when they left that tree, the last link to their father.

(Irma's head pops up from under the table. Her eyes are full of interest. Plum juice runs down her chin and stains her shirt collar.)

IRMA: Do we have a boat?

IBERIA: You know I hate the water. All it's good for is drowning things. Here, take this towel and wipe your face.

(Irma plays with the wet rag, then submits as Iberia rubs the rough cloth over her skin. Her eyes narrow slyly.)

IRMA: Paulette's daddy hit her with his belt the other day. I saw her underpants.

(Iberia's hand flies out.)

IBERIA: I clamp my hand onto Irma's shoulder. I shake her hard. She looks surprised and starts to cry.

I don't want you telling stories and repeating nonsense. Now march to your room and put on a clean shirt before I lose my patience.

(*Irma crawls downstage.*)

Irma didn't speak to me when she came back to the kitchen. She ate dinner in her daddy's lap, except for when she crawled under the table and barked until he fed her biscuits from his hand. I hate it when she acts like a dog, especially at mealtime.

After supper, I go to the porch and watch the weather. Daddy's got to go back to that oil rig in the Gulf, and it looks like a hurricane's coming. I'm ready for this rain to end.

KEELY AND DU
by Jane Martin

Dramatic / 2 Women
> Keely: a pregnant woman taken hostage by a militant anti-abortion organization, 20-30
> Du: the woman assigned by the organization to be her caretaker and companion, 65

The Setting: a basement in Rhode Island, the present

Keely, who was brutally raped by her ex-husband, is kidnapped by right-to-lifers before she can obtain an abortion. She is chained to a bed in a basement and told that she will be forced to carry the child to term. Du is a Bible Christian who cares for Keely. Here, these two very different women begin to find some common ground.

○   ○   ○

(*Lights up on Keely sitting up in bed eating breakfast.*)
DU: (*She watches as Keely eats around the eggs.*) You ever try catsup?
KEELY: What, on eggs?
DU: Oh, we'd buy this spicy kind by the case, Lone Star Catsup. My brothers would heat up the bottles in boiling water so they could get it out faster. (*A moment. Keely pokes at her eggs.*)
KEELY: (*Finally.*) For what?
DU: Eggs, rice, they put it on cantaloupe which like to drove my mother from the house. (*An involuntary smile from Keely, and then, sensing her complicity, silence.*) So, he left high school, Cole?
KEELY: Listen. . .(*Having started to say something about the situation, she thinks better of it, then her need to talk gets the better of her.*) He took a factory job. He was into cars, he wanted this car. His uncle worked a canning line got him on. (*A pause.*)
DU: And?
KEELY: We still went out . . . off and on. We got in an accident,

we were both drunk, I got pretty cut up. My dad's cop pals leaned on him. After that . . . I don't know, lost touch. (*A pause.*)

DU: Lost touch.

KEELY: I don't want to get comfortable talking to you.

DU: Keely . . .

KEELY: Forget it.

DU: Please . . .

KEELY: I said forget it. (*A long pause.*) I'm going crazy in here. I could chew off my wrist here. That paint smear on the pipe up there, I hate that, you know? This floor. That long crack. Everywhere I look. Wherever I look, it makes me sick. (*She tears up.*) Come on, give me a break, will you. I gotta get out of here, I can't do this. (*Mad at herself.*) Damn it.

DU: (*Gently.*) Help us pass the time, Keely. You're not giving up. I know that. (*Keely looks down.*) You lost touch.

KEELY: Yeah. (*A pause.*) There were guys at school, you know, different crowds . . . 37 days, right? (*Du nods.*) I wa . . . man . . . I was, umm, waitressing, actually before he left, down at the Gaslight . . . he didn't like me working. I just blew him off. (*A moment.*) If I talk, it's just talk . . . only talk, that's all . . . because this is shit, what you do to me, worse than that.

DU: Only talk.

KEELY: Because I don't buy this, you tell him I don't buy it. (*Du nods. They sit. Then . . .*) So I was at a Tammy Wynette concert, you know, somebody else's choice, and there he was, definitely his choice as I found out, and my date is . . . well, forget him, so we got together and it got hot really fast and we ended up getting married, which nobody I knew thought was a good idea, which made me really contrary which is a problem I have . . . like up to here . . . so, you know, what I said, we got married, plus . . . (*Finishing the eggs.*) The catsup's all right.

DU: Oh, it's good.

KEELY: I mean I knew who he was, and I did it anyway. I knew about the drinking, I knew about the temper, I don't know where my head was, in my pants, I guess.

DU: Well, I married a man deemed suitable and that can be another problem. There is only one way a man is revealed, and that is day in and day out. You can know a woman through what she says, but don't try it with a man.

KEELY: Yeah, he had a line. I even knew it was a line.

DU: I'll just take the tray.

KEELY: And I knew he drank. Oh, hey, he downpedaled it before we got married . . . way, way downpedaled. He would drink, say two, two drinks, say that was his limit, take me home, go out pour it down 'til ten in the morning, I found that out.

DU: They talk about drugs, but it's still drinking the majority of it, now I have never been drunk in my life, is that something? I'm often tempted so I'll know what I'm missing, yes ma'am, I've tried the marijuana.

KEELY: Bull.

DU: Oh I have, and it didn't do a thing for me, and that's a fact, and I've been in a men's room which I doubt you have, and I've kissed three men in one day, so don't you think you can lord it over me.

KEELY: You smoked?

DU: Oh, yes. Found the marijuana in my son's sock, sat on his bed, waiting 'til I heard him come in the front door, lit up and let him come on up and find me there doing it. Shocked him down to his drawers I might say . . . straightened him up in a hurry. That's the one who's an accountant in Denver. All boys, I would have given my heart for a girl baby. (*An awkward pause.*) It's noisy, too many boys in a house.

KEELY: (*A pause.*) Suitable?

DU: What? Oh, suitable. I was keeping company with a slaughterhouse man who could pop your eyes out with his shirt off, but he was an atheist and a socialist and who knows what else, and that was one too many for my father so he ran him off and put me together with a nice German milkman whose father owned the dairy, if you see my point. August. His name, not the month. I married him at nineteen, in 1947 and two months later the dairy went under, so I got no money and he looked just terrible undressed. The fact is he was an uninteresting man, but he got into the storage business and turned out a good provider. Now, listen close here, we went along 'til he bored me perfectly silent, if you can imagine, and God found us pretty late when the kids were gone or near gone, and God found that man he turned him into a firebrand and an orator and a beacon to others, and I fell in love with him and that bed turned into a lake of flame and I was, so help me, bored no more, and that's a testimony. There is change possible where you never hope to find it, and that is the moral of my story, you can stop listening.

KEELY: Right.

DU: It is. Still nothing to look at but I just close my eyes. The children kept me in that marriage until it became a marriage and the love I bore them kept me alive until the marriage could catch up.

KEELY: So what am I supposed to be? Glad?

DU: Things do change.

KEELY: Yeah, they get worse. He drank more, he got meaner, he screwed around, got herpes, gave 'em to me. My dad got shot, Cole wanted to move to Arizona because he knew I'd have to take care of him. Pawned a lot of stuff, got himself a recliner. I'm waitressing, minimum wage, cashier at a car wash, 70 hours minimum, he drinks himself out of his job, real thoughtful, right? The recession came on, we just fought minute to minute anytime we laid eyes on each other, I said I wanted a divorce, he hit me, and I left. I was out of there 15 minutes after he hit me . . . I was a crazy, out-of-my-mind lunatic I lived with him all that time. Jesus! What the hell was I thinking of?

DU: It was a marriage, Keely.

KEELY: Yeah. After that, he was all over me. I'd look out the window, he'd be in the back yard. The grocery, the library, when I was hanging up laundry, walk into the same bar when I was on a date. He'd come down to the restaurant, say it was about borrowing money, but he knew I wasn't giving him money, forget that, he just liked me to be scared which is what I figured out. Then it stopped for six months, who knows why, then he came back, sent flowers, left messages, begged me to talk to him for one hour so I invited him over, you know, I thought we could sit down and let go of it. I thought I could take his hand and say we're clear, we're two different people. You know, some dumb ass idea like that. That we could just let it go, you know, be whole and be gone, you know what I mean? So I fixed him dinner, and he brought me this stuffed animal, and we were doing, well, not perfect but all right, and I just touched his arm so he would know it was alright, and he locked onto my hand, and I said "let go now," and he started in . . . said he needed . . . pulled me in, you know, hard, and I got a hand in his face, and he . . . he bit down . . . bit down hard, and I . . . I don't know, went nuts . . . bunch of stuff . . . got me down on the floor . . . got me down on the floor and raped me. That's how he caught up with our marriage, that's how he changed. (*They sit in silence.*)

DU: Change can start anytime.

KEELY: I don't want to talk about it. (*A pause.*) You believe God sees you?

DU: I do.

KEELY: He sees you now?

DU: I believe he does. (*A pause.*) Keely? (*No answer.*) Doctor says you're in as good a fourth month as you can be.

KEELY: Let's give it a rest, okay?

DU: He says that baby is lively. (*No response.*) Almost time for your birthday. (*A pause.*)

KEELY: How do you know that?

DU: Now, Keely, that's the least of what I know, and you know it.

KEELY: From my driver's license.

DU: The man says you can have a cake.

KEELY: The man?

DU: The man in charge. (*A moment.*)

KEELY: If I do what, I can have a cake.

DU: Oh, a few pamphlets.

KEELY: I'm not reading that crap, I mean it. Don't you bring it anywhere near me.

DU: You're not afraid of information, are you, honey?

KEELY: You call that information.

DU: Well, there's facts to it.

KEELY: I'm not having a baby. I'm not having it and have somebody adopt it. I'm not having it and keeping it. It won't be. It won't. (*A pause.*)

DU: What would you like for your birthday, honey? (*Keely looks at her.*) Besides that. That's not in my power. (*A pause. Will Keely speak?*)

KEELY: I would like to get dressed. I never liked being in a nightgown. I don't like my own smell. I know that's crazy. You know how you can smell yourself off your night stuff.

DU: Oh, I can share that. That's something that doesn't get a bit better with age, let me tell you.

KEELY: I want to stand up. I want my hands free, I don't care if it's for ten minutes, one minute. I want to walk into a bathroom. I want a chocolate cake. I want to stand up, not bent over on my birthday.

DU: Oh, honey. We only do this because we don't know what else to do. We can't think what else . . . I don't know, I don't . . . birthdays when they're little, the looks on those faces . . . those little hands . . .

KEELY: Little hands, little faces, you make me sick . . . Jesus, can you listen to yourself? All this crap about babies. You don't care about this baby, you just want it to be your little . . . I don't know . . . your little political something, right, God's little visual aid you can hold up at abortion clinics instead of those pickled miscarriages you usually tote around . . . hold up, Baby Tia, wasn't that the one you had downtown trying to pass it off like it was aborted? I can't believe you don't make yourself sick . . . throw up . . . you make me sick, how do you talk this garbage?

DU: (*A moment.*) I have that dress you had on . . . something the worse for wear . . . he might let me get it cleaned . . . cleaned for your birthday. (*A moment.*)

KEELY: I don't hate babies, if that's what you think.

DU: I know that.

KEELY: What the hell is your name? You can . . . you can . . . you can give me that for my birthday. I would like to know what the hell to call you when I talk to you!

DU: Du.

KEELY: What?

DU: I get called Du.

KEELY: Du.

DU: Uh-huh.

KEELY: Du what? Du why? Never mind, forget it . . . I would like to be free for ten minutes on my birthday.

DU: You might have to read some pamphlets.

KEELY: What the hell happened to you, Du? Do you see where we are? Look at this where you got to. Look at me. You used to be a person sometime, right? You look like one. You sound like one. You see the movie Alien where they end up with snakes in their chests? What happened to you?

DU: They tear apart the babies, they poison them with chemicals, and burn them to death with salt solution, they take them out by Caesarean alive and let them die of neglect or strangulation, and then later on, these poor women, they cut their wrists or swallow lye, and then they bring themselves to me because I'm the nurse. Over and over. Over and over. Little hands. Little feet. I've held babies. I've lost babies. I took a baby through six months of chemotherapy and lost that baby. I need to sleep. That's what happened to me.

KEELY: (*Almost gently.*) I can't raise this baby, Du. I'm so angry and fucked up, I just can't do it. I dream of how it happened over and over all the time. I'd be angry at the baby, I think so. I'd hurt the baby sometime and might not even know it, that could happen. If I had a baby, my first one, and I gave it away, I'd just cry all the time, I would. I'm doing this on empty and, if I did that, I would be past empty and I don't know. I have such black moods, it frightens me. The baby would come out of being chained to a bed, you know what I mean. It's not my baby, it's the people's who made me have it, and I couldn't treat it as my baby, not even if I loved it, I couldn't. He'd come around, see. He wouldn't stay off if I had his baby. He would never, ever in this world leave off me, and I think sometime he'll kill me, that's all I can think. Or hurt the baby, whatever, however in his head he could get me, he would do . . . would do it. Really. And I can't have his baby . . . uh . . . it's just not something I can do . . . because I'm about this far, you know . . . right up to the edge of it . . . right there . . . right there. (*A pause.*) So I guess it's me or the baby, so I guess that's crazy, but you don't . . . I don't show you . . . just how . . . how angry I really am. I don't. I don't. (*A pause.*)

DU: He could have changed, Keely. (*A pause. The lights fade.*)

THE LINE THAT PICKED UP 1000 BABES (AND HOW IT CAN WORK FOR YOU)
by Eric Berlin

Serio-Comic / 2 Women
Fran & Ellen: 2 women hanging out in a singles bar, 20-30

The Setting: a singles bar

Gregarious Ellen has dragged Fran out to a singles bar for her birthday. Here, Fran tries to convince Ellen that she'd rather go somewhere else.

O   O   O

ELLEN: You look so *glum*, already. I said I'm sorry. Really.
FRAN: I'm not upset, okay? Just stop.
ELLEN: I forgot your birthday.
FRAN: So. So what? It's no crime. And it's no big deal.
ELLEN: Well, happy birthday anyway.
FRAN: Thanks again.
ELLEN: And I'm sorry.
FRAN: There's nothing to be sorry for.
ELLEN: I *knew* it last week. It buzzed through my mind. And then I forgot until just today.
FRAN: It's okay.
ELLEN: I was at work, standing over the photocopying machine, and it hit me, *Oh my God*!, it's your birthday. And I made a note to get you a card on the way home . . .
FRAN: But you forgot. It's *okay*. It's no big deal.
ELLEN: But what happened was, Eddie, that guy at work with the blue eyes who I was seeing for a while but then he dropped me for whatzername, the one who always wears those short short skirts even in winter? *He* comes by and wants to know if I want to go out sometime, and I said, "Out for *what*?" and he said not to be like that, that he had made a mistake and that we should go out and try to start over. He wants to take things slowly. He doesn't want to go as fast. I always wonder where guys think the speedometer is on these relationships.

So I said I'd think about it, and he said he'd call me, and you know, I think I'm going to go out with him again. Why not? I mean, if he wants to take things slowly then there's nothing to worry about, right?

FRAN: I guess.

ELLEN: So when that all happened, I forgot . . . I'm sorry.

FRAN: It's okay. Just forget about it.

ELLEN: You need to learn how to drop hints better. When my birthday is coming I take out advertising in the newspaper.

FRAN: I don't want to have to remind people.

ELLEN: It's better than having them forget.

FRAN: It doesn't matter.

ELLEN: Don't be a martyr. You deserve to be upset. I'd kill you if you forgot mine. (*Pause.*) If you're going to be upset, *be upset.*

FRAN: *I don't WANT to be upset.* OKAY?

ELLEN: Okay, okay. I really am sorry. But, look, I'm taking you out right? Here we are.

FRAN: Yeah. Here we are. Your favorite bar.

ELLEN: You wanted to come here.

FRAN: No. I didn't.

ELLEN: Then why'd you come when I asked?

FRAN: When you *asked*? You didn't *ask*. You practically put a leash on me and dragged me here.

ELLEN: What's the matter with this place?

FRAN: Nothing . . .

ELLEN: What? What is it?

FRAN: I really don't like standing around here watching guys try to pick you up.

ELLEN: Oh come on.

FRAN: Don't start.

ELLEN: You act as if I get all this *attention*.

FRAN: You do!

ELLEN: You act as if you get *none*.

FRAN: I *don't*.

ELLEN: They try to pick you up too, don't give me that.

FRAN: They pick me up and move me out of the way so they can get to you.

ELLEN: Oh come *on*.

FRAN: It's true and you know it. Why else *would* this be your favorite bar?

ELLEN: . . . it has good drinks.

FRAN: Whaaat?

ELLEN: It *does.*

FRAN: All you drink is beer. You can get the same beer in Shop-Rite.

ELLEN: Well, that's my favorite supermarket.

FRAN: Can't we just go? We've been here long enough.

ELLEN: Hey. See? Look. That guy's looking at you.

FRAN: Oh, sorry. I must be blocking his view of you.

ELLEN: No, *look.* See?

FRAN: . . . how can you possibly tell what he's looking at? This bar is so dark, I can't even see you.

ELLEN: He *is,* I swear.

FRAN: I hope you're someone I know.

ELLEN: You can tell what people are looking at with a little practice.

FRAN: Okay, so he's looking in this *direction.* He's got to be looking somewhere.

ELLEN: And he's choosing to look at you . . . he's kinda cute. . .

FRAN: How can you *tell? You* can't tell what he looks like from here. . .

ELLEN: So go over there and see for yourself.

FRAN: I don't want to go over there. I didn't want to come into the bar in the first place, I certainly don't want to go exploring it.

ELLEN: Fine, fine.

FRAN: So can we go please? Let that be my birthday present.

ELLEN: I bet he comes over here. He's *definitely* looking, kiddo.

FRAN: Guy must have eyes like a fucking hawk.

ELLEN: Just stay until he comes over here.

FRAN: How do you know he will.

ELLEN: Trust me.

FRAN: Oh, Jesus.

ELLEN: I just want to show you that you get more attention than you think you do.

FRAN: I don't want that proved to me.

ELLEN: I'm going to give you your birthday present. Self-esteem.

FRAN: This is terrible! Listen to yourself! I'm going to have self-esteem if some sleazy guy in a bar tries to pick me up? You'll have to excuse me, but I don't make the connection!

ELLEN: You know what it means when a guy picks you up?

FRAN: *Tries* to.

ELLEN: Tries to?

FRAN: What?

ELLEN: You see, guys are real self-conscious. So there has to be a real motivating force if they're going to attempt a discourse with a member of the opposite sex. Exterior beauty is the most obvious exterior force. There's no doubt you've got a great personality, but it is the *exterior attractiveness* that's going to get the key in the lock –

FRAN: So to speak.

ELLEN: – so when strangers start talking to you in bars, it's a compliment, see?

FRAN: Psychology majors should be shot upon graduation.

ELLEN: You disagree?

FRAN: I agree, I agree. I didn't understand anything you said, but if it makes you happy, I'll agree.

ELLEN: Do you *dis*agree?

FRAN: I just said I agree.

ELLEN: Okay . . .

FRAN: Now can we go?

ELLEN: No! How are you going to know otherwise?

FRAN: Know what?

ELLEN: What he thinks of you?

FRAN: I don't *care* what he thinks of me! Who the hell is *he*? We're standing in the same building so that means he's allowed to pass judgment on whether I'm a part of the human race or not?

ELLEN: So fine, sit there and be lonely.

FRAN: I'm not lonely. I'm *alone*.

ELLEN: *Fran*. They're the same thing.

THE OLD LADY'S GUIDE TO SURVIVAL
by Mayo Simon

Dramatic / 2 Women
> Netty and Shprintzy: two old ladies clinging to one another
> for friendship, love and survival, 70-80

The Setting: an apartment in San Diego, the present

Shprintzy is very senile and incapable of caring for herself. When
her daughter with whom she lives commits suicide, she goes to
Netty, her only friend, for help.

O   O   O

NETTY: You're back.
SHPRINTZY: Yeah.
NETTY: (*Suddenly alarmed, jumping up.*) *How did you get in?*
SHPRINTZY: Door was open.
NETTY: What am I coming to? I don't even lock my door
anymore.
(*Trying to regain her composure.*)
So, Shprintzy – what do you want?
SHPRINTZY: (*After a moment, pointing to the memorial candle.*)
The-the-the . . .
NETTY: For my mother.
SHPRINTZY: Oh . . .
NETTY: Did you want something?
SHPRINTZY: You-you seeing the little letters any better?
NETTY: A little better, thank you . . . Are you going to say
something?
SHPRINTZY: (*Starting to wander slowly.*) Say something . . .
NETTY: About what? About your daughter?
(*Shprintzy nods.*)
Did you talk to her?
SHPRINTZY: Oh, sure.
NETTY: Did you stand up for yourself? Did you tell her nobody
steps on you because you don't allow it?
SHPRINTZY: Yeah.

NETTY: What did she say?

SHPRINTZY: Nothing.

NETTY: Nothing? What did you do?

SHPRINTZY: I took the bus. I went to the JCC. There was dancing . . .

NETTY: And then?

SHPRINTZY: Came back.

NETTY: *And?*

SHPRINTZY: . . . The manager of the . . .

NETTY: What manager?

SHPRINTZY: . . . the manager of the. . .

NETTY: Complex?

(*Shprintzy nods.*)

What about him?

SHPRINTZY: . . . told me . . .

NETTY: Told you what?

SHPRINTZY: . . . There was a note . . .

NETTY: What note?

(*Shprintzy stares at her.*)

What note?

SHPRINTZY: She left a note.

NETTY: Your daughter left you a note? What did she say?

SHPRINTZY: She went away.

NETTY: Where did she go?

(*No answer.*)

Moved out? Took her things?

SHPRINTZY: Gone.

NETTY: Well, now you'll have a nice big apartment to yourself.

SHPRINTZY: And a cat.

NETTY: A cat too?

(*A dubious expression.*)

Well, that's very nice . . . So where did she go, your daughter?

SHPRINTZY: To the store.

NETTY: The store? You said she went away.

SHPRINTZY: She went down to the store . . . She told the man she was going hunting . . . She wanted something to go hunting . . .

NETTY: Oh, no . . .

SHPRINTZY: And then she came back . . .

NETTY: Oh, no . . .

SHPRINTZY: . . . into my room . . .

NETTY: Oh, no . . .

SHPRINTZY: . . . and put it against her . . .

(*Shprintzy points to her heart.*)

NETTY: Oh my God . . .

SHPRINTZY: She left a note. It wasn't a bad note.

NETTY: Oh my God . . .

SHPRINTZY: She couldn't see anything more for her in life . . .

(*Shprintzy turns, starts out.*)

NETTY: Where are you going?

SHPRINTZY: Where?

NETTY: Where are you going to go?

SHPRINTZY: My baby is dead.

(*Shprintzy walks off. Netty stares after her.*)

NETTY: Somebody will take her in . . . Or she'll go home . . . She has a nice home . . . A nice apartment, nicer than mine.

(*Hands to her face, rocks back and forth in anguish*.)

I can't help her. I can't let myself be dragged down. I can't . . .

(*Suddenly she calls out*)

Shprintzy!

(*Shprintzy reappears.*)

SHPRINTZY: Where's the front door? Did you move it?

(*Netty stares at Shprintzy.*)

NETTY: Shprintzy, why don't you sit down.

SHPRINTZY: I was in the closet. I got lost.

(*Shprintzy laughs.*)

NETTY: Sit down.

(*Shprintzy sits at the table. Netty sits across from her. She takes her hand. The scene goes to black.*)

THE POWER AND THE GLORY
by Le Wilhelm

Serio-Comic / 2 Women
 Inez & Wanda: two friends taking a ride in an elevator, 30-40

The Setting: a glass elevator, the present

Inez has talked Wanda into taking a ride in an elevator for some much needed therapy. As the glassed-in lift rises higher and higher, Inez reveals her true intent.

O   O   O

INEZ: Look down there.

WANDA: I can't.

INEZ: Yes, you can. Just take your time. We'll just push the hold button. Now, look down there, Wanda. It's important. Look. There you go.

WANDA: It's so far down.

INEZ: Yes, so far down. See all those little insect people down there.

WANDA: So small.

INEZ: Hundreds of men down there. Men of all races. Men from all over. Hundreds of men.

WANDA: There are women there, too.

INEZ: We don't care about the women. Just the men. And there's hundreds of them.

WANDA: And not one wants me.

INEZ: Wrong. Look again, Wanda.

WANDA: I see them, Inez.

INEZ: Now did you do like I told you?

WANDA: Yes.

INEZ: You're not wearing any underwear and no pantyhose, right?

WANDA: No, I'm not, but I think that's the craziest thing I ever heard of. I was afraid to sit down on the subway. Going around in a skirt without panties on – I think you're making a fool out of me.

INEZ: I'm not wearing any, either.

WANDA: Maybe you are and maybe you aren't.

INEZ: I'll show you.

WANDA: I believe you, Inez. Goodness.

INEZ: Now look close at those men down there, Wanda. What are they doing?

WANDA: They're going about their jobs, going to work, going to stores. I don't know what all of them are doing. Just walking around.

INEZ: No, Wanda.

WANDA: What are they doing?

INEZ: They're slowing down, Wanda. They're barely moving. They're almost at a standstill. Do you know why?

WANDA: They're waiting for the light to change?

INEZ: No, Wanda. They're looking up our dresses.

WANDA: (*Grabbing and tucking.*) They're what?

INEZ: They're looking up our dresses. That's why we didn't wear any underwear.

WANDA: That's dirty, Inez.

INEZ: It's life, Wanda.

WANDA: They can't see anything this far up.

INEZ: Wrong, Wanda. When men are looking up women's dresses, their eyes are like those of an eagle.

WANDA: Oh, for goodness sake.

INEZ: They are. Stand a little closer to the glass, Wanda. Lift your skirt a little, spread your legs, let them see all the way up your dress.

WANDA: I most certainly will not!! Lord knows what kind of men are down there.

INEZ: All kinds of men. All kinds of men from all over the world. The rich, the poor, the religious, the infidels. The lovers, the haters, they're all there, and now (*She stands and tilts her dress.*) they are all looking up my dress.

WANDA: You'll get us arrested!

INEZ: By the police? They're looking, too! They're all looking up my dress, adoring me!! Tilt your skirt, Wanda, let them see your power.

WANDA: It's against the law –

INEZ: We're not exposing ourselves, Wanda. We've got dresses on. It's not our fault if they want to look.

WANDA: It's nasty.

INEZ: No, it's life!! It's eternity!

WANDA: It's ridiculous.

INEZ: Don't you want to feel good about yourself? Don't you want to feel like a worthy human being? Don't you want the power?

WANDA: I don't think of my na na as power.

INEZ: That's a big mistake, Wanda, cause it is. It's the most powerful thing in the world. Come on, Wanda, let them see your power.

WANDA: I feel like a fool.

INEZ: You'll learn to love it. It's just the two of us, Wanda.

WANDA: (*Weakening.*) Inez –

INEZ: Step up, tilt your skirt. Try it, Wanda. Please, you won't regret it.

WANDA: Alright. (*Very gingerly does so.*)

INEZ: Just stand there. Think of all those men from all over. Close your eyes and see them. Men from all over America. There are Japanese, Chinese, Malaysians, Frenchmen, Englishmen, Irishmen, Germans, Poles, Russkies, Zairians, Zimbabweans, Zanzabarians, Togoians, maybe even Outer Mongolians. All these men of the world pass along the street, and Wanda, they're all looking. They're looking, and they see where they were created. They see and they long for the place they began. Feel their gaze.

WANDA: I do, and I'm not sure I like it.

INEZ: They're adoring us, Wanda. (*Her fervor is getting very high.*) Adoring us, we are the thing in which all humankind is created. We possess the cauldron. We are the survival of the species. We are the house of creation, the temple of God, the instrument of the goddess. We are all of that, Wanda. Feel them look, feel them adore, feel them desire. Take pity on them. Let their gaze penetrate your body.

WANDA: I'm feeling very warm, Inez.

INEZ: It's the power. The power. The energy. Wars have been fought over us. All things that exist come from us. The power is surging. Let it fill your body. Feel it, Wanda. You are the power. They adore you. Say it, Wanda. Say, "I am the power." Come on, Wanda.

WANDA: I am the power.

INEZ: Humankind springs from me.

WANDA: Humankind springs from me.

INEZ: Creation occurs inside me.

WANDA: Creation occurs inside me.

INEZ: I am woman!! All powerful.

WANDA: I am all powerful woman. You're right, Inez. They are looking. I can feel it. They want me. They want me BAD. AND I LOVE IT. DID YOU HEAR ME, INEZ, I LOVE IT. LOVE, LOVE, LOVE IT. LOOK AT ME, ALL YOU PUNY LITTLE MEN. LOOK AT ME AND LOVE ME. SEE MY NA NA. SEE MY NA NA AND SHAKE WITH DESIRE. YES. YES. YES. YES.

INEZ: You don't want to overdo, Wanda.

WANDA: Love me. LOVE ME. DO YOU HEAR ME? LOVE ME. I AM THE POWER. I AM THE GLORY. FALL ON YOUR KNEES AND WORSHIP ME. I FEEL YOUR DESIRE RISING UPWARD. RISING UPWARD, AND I AM READY FOR IT. I AM WANDA THE WONDERFUL!!

INEZ: (*Frightened.*) Wanda, the elevator's beginning to shake.

WANDA: CAN"T YOU FEEL IT, INEZ? CAN'T YOU FEEL THEIR DESIRE? FEEL IT PENETRATE!!!

INEZ: WANDA!! WANDA, YOU'VE GOT TO GET A HOLD OF YOURSELF!

WANDA: Oh, yes, yes, yes, yes, yes. YES, YES, YES, YES. OHHHHHHHHHHHHHHHHHH!

INEZ: Wanda!!

WANDA: What, Inez?

INEZ: Calm down. That's enough.

WANDA: Just a little more. I was really depressed.

INEZ: I know you were, but there's a limit to what they can take.

WANDA: Inez, I am the instrument of creation.

INEZ: That's what I have been trying to tell you.

WANDA: All power springs from me.

INEZ: Yes, and remember Wanda, whenever you get blue or down, you can always come here and take a ride in this glass elevator.

WANDA: It's better than any shrink, Inez!!

INEZ: And it won't go away for a long time. You're going to feel great for the next week or more.

WANDA: You think so?

INEZ: I know it. Every time I come here and get recharged, men won't leave me alone for days.

WANDA: I'm ready.

INEZ: We'd better get going, Wanda.

WANDA: Inez, do you think we could do one more charge up as the elevator goes down?

INEZ: Couldn't do any harm, but don't get too carried away, Wanda.

WANDA: I won't. Inez, I want to thank you for this.

INEZ: Don't mention it, Wanda.

(*They hold their dresses out as they descend and we hear "Amazing Grace." The end.*)

REMEMBRANCE
by Graham Reid

Dramatic / 2 Women

    Deirdre: a woman struggling to keep it together while her
         IRA husband serves a prison sentence, 30-40
    Joan: her unmarried sister, 30s

The Setting: Northern Ireland, the present

Deirdre is tired of visiting her husband in prison. She is also tired
of going to bed alone every night. She longs for warmth and
companionship, as she here tells her sister over tea.

O   O   O

DEIRDRE: You're going to have those brasses rubbed away
    before you're done.
JOAN: Where are the children?
DEIRDRE: At school . . . summer play scheme. Where's my ma?
JOAN: She went up to the cemetery.
DEIRDRE: It's not healthy the way you two live. She has that
    grave like a well-kept window box and you've the house like
    an operating theatre. A wee bit of dirt's human you know,
    shows a place is lived in.
JOAN: How do you know what the grave looks like? You never
    go up.
DEIRDRE: I can guess. (*Pause.*)
JOAN: (*Glancing up at Deirdre.*) Are you visiting Joe today?
DEIRDRE: I'd better, otherwise the bastards won't give me any
    money.
JOAN: If you were a Protestant you could divorce him.
DEIRDRE: If I was a Protestant I wouldn't have married him in the
    first place.
JOAN: You shouldn't have married him anyway. I never liked him.
DEIRDRE: It's a pity about you. I didn't care what you thought. It
    was love. He swept me off my feet.
JOAN: I think you were in love with the idea of being in love. I
    never knew anybody as desperate to get married.

DEIRDRE: I'd all these daft notions . . . me, the contented little home-maker, him out knocking his pan in to keep me in a befitting style. The lazy frigger couldn't have worked to keep himself warm . . . and mine was the only pan he knocked in! (*Pause. Looks at Joan. Considers.*) Have you ever screwed, Joan?
(*Joan???*)
You know, had sex.

JOAN: I know what it means. What's it got to do with you?

DEIRDRE: I'd love a man. What am I supposed to do for the rest of my life?

JOAN: Maybe he'll get out. Maybe there'll be an amnesty.

DEIRDRE: I don't want him, though. For Christ's sake don't say any of this to my ma. (*Pause.*) Maybe it's just this hot weather. They watch me you know.

JOAN: Who does?

DEIRDRE: His mates. The women of Ireland must not be enjoying themselves when their men are serving time for the cause. (*Pause, Upset.*) I think I'm going mad.

JOAN: Why don't you put the teapot on?

DEIRDRE: I'm sexually frustrated, emotionally deprived, severely depressed . . . not thirsty.

JOAN: You need a holiday.

DEIRDRE: Thanks, Joan, you've been a great help.

JOAN: Sorry.

DEIRDRE: Life has to have more for me than this. I'll be an old woman by the time he gets out. I want a life. I deserve a life.

JOAN: You've got the children.

DEIRDRE: Oh yes, great. Five, six, and seven. As close together as the bastard could put them. Only for the RUC I'd probably be the mother of seven, with an eighth on the way.

JOAN: I thought you loved the kids?

DEIRDRE: (*Shouting.*) Of course I love the fucking kids. (*Pause.*) Sorry, sorry, love. (*Pause.*) The latest in birth control . . . a three a.m. arrest and a life sentence. Now some well-meaning idiots want to let them screw us at visiting time . . . marvelous!

JOAN: Do you talk to Joe about it?

DEIRDRE: I don't talk to Joe about anything. I listen to Joe, about Joe. You know it's not really the man who serves the life sentence. Christ, sometimes I think capital punishment wouldn't be a bad thing. At least we'd be free to start again. (*Pause.*) Put that teapot on, love, will you?

JOAN: (*Rising. Concerned.*) Sit down . . . relax. (*Goes and puts the teapot on.*) . . . that'll not take a minute. (*Starts replacing the brasses.*) You know you should see the doctor.

DEIRDRE: Right enough, even he'd do . . . anything in trousers. (*Pause.*) Sometimes I think I've woken up in the wrong lifetime. I should go back to being a dog, or a frog, or whatever I was before. Mind you, with my luck, I was probably Dr. Crippen's wife. (*Pause.*) I woke up feeling very randy this morning.

(*Joan looks disapprovingly.*)

Don't look at me like that. You just don't realize. Nobody does. The kids were kicking up a racket and I wanted to hear a man's voice telling them to behave. I wanted to reach an arm out and touch someone.

JOAN: Don't you think it's hard for him too?

DEIRDRE: Yes, of course. We should never forget the guilty.

JOAN: I thought you believed in all of that?

DEIRDRE: Today I believe in me. Mother Ireland will have to take a back seat.

JOAN: I promised you tea.

DEIRDRE: Yes . . . as a substitute for all that's missing in my life.

JOAN: There's some bread, brown or white. Men we don't supply.

DEIRDRE: Talking of which, when are you going to . . .

JOAN: Don't! I claim one day free from the "you need a nice young man" routine.

DEIRDRE: A "nice" young man's the last thing you need. He'd probably sit helping you clean those damned brasses.

JOAN: It's good therapy. I need to be doing something.

DEIRDRE: We're all in the same boat, aren't we? I mean life is a life sentence, isn't it? Don't you think so? I mean hobbies, chores, duties, responsibilities . . . they're all ways of helping us get through a life sentence, aren't they?

JOAN: (*Pondering. Playful.*) No . . . maybe . . . yes and yes!

DEIRDRE: (*Nasty.*) I don't know why, with your decisiveness, your life's fell apart. (*Pause.*) I'm sorry. Oh Christ, what am I doing? I'm a mess Joan. It's one of those days. Every so often I realize the significance of that emptiness on the other side of the bed.

(*Joan looks at her sympathetically.*)

SERPENT IN THE NIGHT
by Dianne Warren

Serio-Comic / 3 Women
> Joy: engaged to Duff, whom she met while hitchhiking, 17
> Stella: Duff's abrasive and pregnant sister, 20s
> Marlene: Stella and Duff's mother; a survivalist who chooses
> to live in the woods, 55

The Setting: a small town in Saskatchewan, the present

Duff has left Joy with Stella, the sister who raised him when their mother left to live in the wild, while he goes on a fishing trip with Gator, Stella's husband. While they wait for the men to return, they are paid an unexpected visit by Marlene. Stella is very angry with Marlene, and before long the two argue, leaving poor Joy stuck in the middle.

O   O   O

JOY: Duff said they'd be back.

STELLA: That means a lot. We all know how reliable Duff is.

MARLENE: Look, Stella. You can give me my truck another time. Tomorrow. After you get things straightened out with Gator.

STELLA: It's never going to be straightened out with Gator. I'd like to kill him. I buy the thing and the next day he makes off with it. Will you sit down, Marlene?

MARLENE: I don't think they're coming.

JOY: Duff said they'd be back.

STELLA: Would you rather have a trailer? I was going to buy you a trailer.

MARLENE: (*Working her way to the door.*) I don't want a trailer, Stella. Don't need a truck either, for that matter. I like to walk.

STELLA: Walk.

MARLENE: Yes, walk.

STELLA: Just where the hell do you walk to, Marlene? You were gone for a whole year last time. A year. Nobody goes for a walk and stays gone for a year.

MARLENE: I go . . . places. Just places.

STELLA: Places!

MARLENE: I need to walk.

STELLA: Like right now.

MARLENE: What?

STELLA: You're trying to get out of here, Marlene. Don't think I can't see it. How long will you be gone this time? Two years? Ten? You could at least give me the chance to give you the God-damned truck.

MARLENE: I need to walk.

STELLA: That's the craziest excuse I've ever heard for being a bad mother.

MARLENE: It's not that I don't think about you.

STELLA: Oh, well that makes it okay then.

MARLENE: You make out just fine without me.

STELLA: Yeah. Fine. I make out fine. And what about Duff? Is he fine?

MARLENE: Duff?

STELLA: Yeah. Duff. Your son, remember?

MARLENE: He's healthy. A big strapping . . .

STELLA: (*Interrupting.*) He hangs around with Gator.

MARLENE: Duff's young. There's still time.

STELLA: Time for what?

MARLENE: Well, time for . . . I don't know. Time.

STELLA: Time. Well, go ahead. Leave. Go for your walk. See if I care. Go. Get out of here. Gator can keep your truck. I don't care. (*Pause.*) He hates you, you know?

MARLENE: What?

STELLA: Duff. He hates you. He can't stand you.

MARLENE: He doesn't hate me.

STELLA: He thinks you're crazy. He can't stand even to hear your name.

MARLENE: I'm his mother.

STELLA: I'm his mother, Marlene. Me. You know what he tells people? He tells them his real mother died.

MARLENE: Everybody knows I'm his mother.

STELLA: In a . . . a plane crash. When he was a baby.

MARLENE: That's a lie.

STELLA: That's what he tells people.

JOY: That's not true, Stella.

STELLA: (*To Marlene.*) Go on. Get out of here.

JOY: Don't go, Marlene. Don't. Stay until Duff gets back.

STELLA: He's not coming.

JOY: He wants to see you. I know he does.

STELLA: *You* know. You. What do you know about Duff?

JOY: I don't know very much about Duff. But I don't think you do either.

STELLA: (*To Marlene.*) He hates the ground you walk on.

JOY: I know what you're doing.

STELLA: Do you hear me, Marlene?

JOY: You're just trying to hurt her.

STELLA: What is it with you, you think you know so much? You come in here out of nowhere, and think you can fix people's lives.

JOY: I don't try to fix anybody's life. I don't know how.

STELLA: That's right. You don't know how. You don't know much of anything, Joy.

JOY: I'm not stupid, if that's what you think.

STELLA: No?

JOY: I know more than you think I do.

STELLA: About what?

JOY: About lots of things.

STELLA: Lots of things. Yeah. Cleaning and cooking. And hey. Let's not forget fucking.

JOY: Shut up!

STELLA: You know what I think? I think you *are* stupid. You thought you could come up here and live some kind of life with Duff. That was a really fucking stupid idea.

JOY: At least I'm not going around six months pregnant, expecting people to believe me when I say I'm not!
(*Stella slaps Joy's face. They stare at each other.*)

MARLENE: (*Pause.*) Stella. I'm really glad about the baby.

STELLA: The baby.

MARLENE: I know you've been saying there's no baby. But there is a baby. Anybody can see it.

STELLA: I don't want to talk about it, Marlene.

MARLENE: You'll be a good mother. Won't she, Joy? Won't Stella be a good mother?

JOY: Yes.

MARLENE: She raised Duff. She was a good mother to Duff. (*Hearing something outside.*) What's that?

STELLA: What?

JOY: They came back. Oh. There's somebody with them.

MARLENE: (*Going to window.*) Is that my truck? Say. That is a nice truck, Stella. If I were buying a truck, I'd buy one just like that. I really like . . . that little decal on the door. That's nice. What is it? A deer?

STELLA: Jesus. Yeah, Marlene. It's a deer.

STRANGERS ON EARTH
by Mark O'Donnell

Serio-Comic / 2 Women
   Margaret: a blue collar prodigy, 22
   Priss: a highly strung WASP, 22

The Setting: here and now

On the day of their graduation from Radcliffe, Margaret and Priss share a moment together before they must go and face the rest of their lives.

O   O   O

MARGARET: Honestly, sometimes I am ashamed of you!

PRISS: Please don't torture me. Margaret, I can do that for myself.

MARGARET: (*Removing her gown; she wears casual clothes.*) You are so wishy washy sometimes you're in danger of drowning. How could you do that? Why did you do that?

PRISS: (*Following suit.*) How should I know? Do you think I can read my mind? Come on! Everybody gets sudden memory blocks. Especially around their parents.

MARGARET: Lucky for you John let you off the hook and introduced himself.

PRISS: But we'd broken up months ago, it's not like I was keeping some current truth from them.

MARGARET: You'd think saying his name was like uttering the word penis to them.

PRISS: I don't know what happened, I just was afraid my father's antennae were scanning for intruders! Even liberals are territorial!

MARGARET: And John's being black didn't enter into this the least bit? (*They begin to undress.*)

PRISS: (*Indignantly.*) Now that is a pretty low limbo. Daddy works with a lot of very tall Africans at the Foundation! Just because your family's poor, you're so proud! You think it gives you the right to criticize. (*They change quickly from jeans and pullovers* to *dresses suitable for dinner in a nice restaurant*.) Anyhow – Nobody said a thing!

MARGARET: (*In bursts, as they dress.*) It was the way they didn't say it. It would have been Mock Around the Clock if Brother Teddy had any idea how many of Harvard's flotsam you'd been ministering to! You take the Missionary position as a whole way of life! (*Pause.*) Poor little seven-foot John! (*Beat.*) *There* was a romance made in Purgatory! . . . Oh! – And Ray, the Bard of Coral Gables! That moronic Queen Elizabeth play *you* could have written better! "What I will will will be!" . . . and brr, whatsisname, that physicist! "Donald K. Brown, the K stands for Potassium!" – And a few others who shall remain brainless! . . .

PRISS: I never said I loved them. I just wanted to do what I could for people who needed me.

MARGARET: The mercy date! The one woman foundation! You are a Caucasian's Caucasian! You say you want to write, but you're so full of self-denial!

PRISS: You're making me feel a monster for trying to help people!

MARGARET: People you don't love. Tyrannized by those you pity! Oh, what's the use of trying to talk to you? The ears have walls!

PRISS: (*Hurt enough to retaliate.*) . . . Even if they were just rituals – At least I've *had* dates! (*Margaret is properly stung by this, which Priss regrets.*)

MARGARET: Speaking of low limbos .. I'll have to have that little pointer surgically removed. (*Pause.*) Anyway, I am a tad pickier than you.

PRISS: I'm sorry, Margaret, I know it hurts you that your family didn't come, but you're taking it out on me unfairly. I'd expect a psychology major to have more control!

MARGARET: (*Sheepish.*) Well . . . If I'd majored in Biology, it wouldn't have made me immortal. (*Pause.*) I'm sorry, too. We should be thinking about the future anyway, right? (*Beat.*) Our kamikaze life pact! (*They hug briefly.*)

PRISS: (*Trying to brighten the mood.*) And more immediately, dinner – courtesy the Fairburn Foundation.

MARGARET: Ready?

PRISS: Ready enough. (*She fastens her pearl necklace.*) Am I forgiven?

MARGARET: For what, *my* bad temper? These heels make me feel like I'm Mary getting ready for the Assumption. (*They head out to join Priss' parents and brother.*)

PRISS: Margaret! What do you think tomorrow holds?

MARGARET: I don't think tomorrow holds. I think it drops.

THE VIEW FROM HERE
by Margaret Dulaney

Serio-Comic / 3 Women
> Fern: an agoraphobic, 30s
> Maple: her sister, 30s
> Carla: Fern's neighbor, 30s

The Setting: a home in suburban Kentucky

While visiting her agoraphobic sister, Maple reveals that she and her husband have been trying – unsuccessfully – to have a child for 12 years.

O   O   O

CARLA: Aloha!

FERN: You missed aerobics.

CARLA: Well, pooh.

FERN: What you been doing?

CARLA: Been home tuned into my police scanner. Got a sick feeling something tragic's gonna happen today.

FERN: Why's that?

CARLA: It's the new moon. Read somewhere that the new moon messes up your sense of timing. It's like being in a time warp, see. You could think you were doing 55 when in actuality you're doing 135. Or, maybe someone's signalling for a turn, front of you, and you're thinking you got plenty of time to slow down, but that's just exactly where you're messed up, see, and there's a ten to one chance you'd mow that poor sucker down all on account of its being your new moon . . . Yep . . . I haven't been in a car on the day of the new moon in over three years.

MAPLE: Three years?

CARLA: Hasn't been easy.
(To Fern.)
You still got the Brainard Boys?

FERN: Ellen came to fetch 'em half hour ago.

CARLA: Got anymore coming in?

FERN: Not unless they crawl over here on their own.

CARLA: Maple, honey you got any children?

MAPLE: Nope.

CARLA: You're probably like me, then. I think they're awful cute in the front of someone else's grocery cart, but I'd sooner eat mosquitoes, than birth one.

FERN: Carla. Maple wants a baby so badly, she could spit teardrops.

CARLA: Oh, honey, I'm so sorry! Oh, I can't think of anything more tragic than wanting to be a mama and not being able to. Donahue had a woman on the other day, got so whacked out over not being able to have a baby, went out and stole her one, right out of one of those grocery carts, matter-of-fact, but, before she took it, she made pretty damn sure that kid's parents weren't in any shape to come trotting out after her . . . Mowed 'em down in the grocery store parking lot . . . Tragic . . . Tragic . . . Who is it has the problem, Maple, honey, you or your husband?

MAPLE: What problem?

CARLA: What I mean is, have you been to see anyone about this? Course, I wouldn't blame you if you hadn't. I haven't been to a gynecologist for years, after hearing about that gynecological cult.

MAPLE: What?!

FERN: Carla, you hear about the darndest things!

CARLA: You didn't hear about that? Women would come into this fellow's office, and after just one appointment, they'd be hooked. Brainwashed. Give him anything he asked for, And let me tell you, he performed some procedures on those ladies, made a papsmear sound like a picnic.

MAPLE: Good grief!

CARLA: One woman claimed he . . .

FERN: Carla! I believe this is one story I'd just as soon go to my grave without hearing.

CARLA: Suit yourself.

(*She gives them a knowing look.*)

So, have you two ever been tested?

MAPLE: Oh, we don't believe in all that testing stuff. Figure it's all in our heads. We just haven't found the key, is all.

CARLA: Is that right? How long you been trying?

MAPLE: 'Bout twelve years.

CARLA: Oh, uh-huh . . .

(*Carla looks at Fern. Pause.*)

Guess who I bumped into at the Seven-Eleven, guess . . . Arnold.

FERN: Palmer? How'd he look?

CARLA: Like he'd just got through swallowing his teeth.

FERN: Poor fellow! Guess he'd just been home to see the clean-out job, huh?

CARLA: I wonder did he notice the microwave yet?

FERN: Shoot, I bet he's back over there now trying to club himself senseless with a five iron.

(*The phone rings.*)

Now, this is bound to be Stan.

(*Picks up phone.*) Fern's Factory Outlet, how may I help you? . . . Oh, hello Mama . . . Nope, no relapses. I'd say her jaw is pretty well oiled now . . . listen . . .

(*She holds the phone away from her and quacks.*)

Quack. Quack. Quack.

(*Back to the phone.*)

You plannin' on calling every 25 minutes today? There goes your call-us-interrupt-us . . . How many time's he called? . . . Who's he asking for? . . . NO?! . . . Mama! . . . Mama, don't pick up the phone anymore. That fellow's been calling here too, asking could he speak to Bernice. Called three times . . . Well just . . . Well just don't . . . Just don't pick up the . . . Hung up on me. Good night. This is kinda creepy.

CARLA: That fellow called here three times?

FERN: Yeah.

CARLA: Sign of a rapist.

MAPLE: What?!

CARLA: Fellow in Chicago, raped thirty, forty women. Always used to call his victims up beforehand, asking could he speak to Hilda. Come to find out later that Hilda was his mean old dead mother, and this was his way of getting even, see. I wouldn't sleep here alone tonight, Fern, if my life depended on it.

FERN: That seems awful drastic . . .

MAPLE: You ever heard of "Bernice's Hair"?

CARLA: That that place out on Walnut, pulled that bouffant stunt on me?

FERN: No, what she's talking about is a bunch of stars, looks like hair.

MAPLE: It's a constellation up in the sky.

CARLA: You don't say . . . Hair, up in the sky, huh?

(*Pause.*)

Is it straight or kinky?

FERN: Wouldn't ask that, if I were you.

MAPLE: (*Gives Fern a look.*) Hard to tell.

FERN: What's the point, Maple?

MAPLE: Well . . . Stan . . . thinks that may be the key.

FERN: Bunch of stars?

MAPLE: Not exactly . . . It's a kind of theory . . . something Stan dreamed up around last Christmas . . . he thinks it might help us get pregnant . . . Help me get pregnant. Well, you know what I mean . . .

FERN: No, not exactly, no.

MAPLE: It's just something he dreamed up . . . You know Stan. He's always so full of theories . . . (*Pause.*)

FERN: Are you gonna tell us what it is?

MAPLE: Well . . . It all started last Christmas, when I was opening up my presents . . . Stan says there's one he wants me to save and open last. So, of course I thought it was gonna be a new washer-dryer, or a microwave, or something like that . . .

FERN: Microwave! What time is it?

CARLA: Six fifteen.

FERN: Oh. Sorry, go ahead.

MAPLE: I don't know . . . It's kinda private.

FERN: Oh no, Maple, I'm sorry, go on.

CARLA: Go ahead, hon. It'll never leave this room.

MAPLE: Well . . . It wasn't hardly a microwave.

CARLA: What was it?

MAPLE: Opened it up, pulled out a real, human hair, jet black, wig.

(*Pause while Fern's and Carla's faces are frozen in anticipation.*)

That's how I felt. I tried to freeze my face so it wouldn't move on from the look of surprise it had on it, into what might naturally follow, when Stan says, "Aren't you excited, honey? That's Bernice's Hair. That's gonna be the key to our fertility."

I kept my face frozen with some difficulty.

(*She demonstrates.*)

He goes on to say how maybe the reason we weren't making babies is because somewhere inside of us, we don't believe that Maple can have babies. That Maple is barren. So, if we were to pretend that Maple were someone else, someone like, for instance, Bernice with jet black hair, then, well, maybe Bernice could get herself knocked up.

FERN: Well, I never . . .

CARLA: Got a unique imagination.

FERN: I'll say . . . He have you wear that wig to bed?!

MAPLE: Gosh, Fern, you know we'd do anything to have a baby!

FERN: I guess so!

(*There is an awkward pause.*)

Must have been some Christmas.

CARLA: And here we were, stringing popcorn and cranberries.

FERN: Guess it didn't work, did it?

MAPLE: What?

CARLA: The . . . theory.

MAPLE: 'Spose it still could.

FERN: You still wearing it?!

MAPLE: Gosh, Fern, you know how desperate we are!

FERN: Desperate, yeah!!

MAPLE: (*She gets up and walks over to a corner of the room.*) It's not so bad on. Got it stuffed in this Piggly Wiggly bag.

(*She digs in the bag and pulls out a sad looking black wig and puts it on her head.*)

CARLA: Tragic.

FERN: Maple . . .

(*She can't think of what to say.*)

How long you two gonna give this wig theory?

MAPLE: I don't know . . .

FERN: Maple!

MAPLE: We're desperate!

FERN: Yeah, you mentioned that.

CARLA: Tragic. (*Pause.*)

MAPLE: I got seven different ones now.

FERN: What?

MAPLE: Yeah . . .

(*She dumps more wigs out of the bag on the floor.*)

I'm seven different people now, but for some reason, my name's always Bernice. There's Black-headed Bernice, Blond-headed Bernice, Red-headed Bernice, Brunette Bernice, Long-haired Bernice, Curly-headed Bernice, and bouffant Bernice.

FERN and CARLA: Bouffant?!!

CARLA: Tragic.

FERN: Maple! . . . So, you mean that was Stan calling here asking could he speak to Bernice?!

(*Maple looks at her.*)

Why didn't he ask for Maple, so I'd know who the heck he was talking about. Like to scared me to death!

(*Maple looks like she's gonna cry. Pause.*)

CARLA: I guess it's been a while since he asked for Maple, huh?

(*Pause as all three think about this.*)

Scenes
For Men

ALL FALL DOWN
by Wendy Lill

Dramatic / 2 Men
Connors: a social worker, 30-50
Ewan: a father, 30s

The Setting: an office, the present

Ewan's young son has indicated that he has been sexually abused by his teacher. Here, the crusading Connors tries to convince a disbelieving Ewan to join the fight.

O   O   O

(*Connors is sitting in his office going over papers. Ewan comes to the door.*)
EWAN: I'd like more information.
CONNORS: Sit down.
(*Ewan sits.*)
Your wife talked to you, I assume.
EWAN: Yes.
CONNORS: I can't really tell you any more than what I told her at this point. This is still the accumulation of information stage.
EWAN: (*With difficulty.*) What can you tell me?
CONNORS: With the assistance of an anatomically correct doll, I was able to determine that Annie Boland may have had sexual relations with your son, probably making use of certain articles.
EWAN: (*Finally brings himself.*) What articles?
CONNORS: Peanut butter, popsicle sticks, spoons, dinky toys, possibly playdoh.
EWAN: Playdoh.
CONNORS: Possibly.
(*Ewan jumps up and starts pacing.*)
I know this is a horrible shock. This is new territory. Take your time. I strongly advise my families to seek independent counselling. Parents of abuse cases are secondary victims. Family counselling does help. I've seen some families come out

of this experience even stronger than when they went in.

EWAN: You have?

CONNORS: Yes, I have.

EWAN: Why wouldn't Rory tell me? He tells me about every little fib, every little punch he gives out, every mean thought . . . why wouldn't he tell me about this? If this is in fact true?

CONNORS: Probably because you're so close. He may have thought you'd turn away from him, stop loving him.

EWAN: I would never stop loving him.

CONNORS: Kids don't always know that.

EWAN: And you're sure about this?

CONNORS: As sure as I can be. The evidence is building.

EWAN: I heard about the little girl; that one of your social workers has physical evidence that a little girl's been interfered with as you call it. How do you know who did it? Did she actually say that Annie Boland did it? (*Connors hesitates.*) She didn't say that, did she? You're just speculating. I mean it could have been her father, her brother, couldn't it? Have you yourself ever seen any solid physical evidence linking anything to Annie Boland?

CONNORS: No.

EWAN: Did anyone over four years old witness these so called Acts?

CONNORS: No. (*This does bother him.*) So far there is no adult evidence. There almost never is.

EWAN: And that doesn't worry you?

CONNORS: Of course it worries us, but we believe the truth can be pieced together from the parent and child testimonies. They're like building blocks.

EWAN: You make it sound like a science.

CONNORS: It's a human science, but we can never be 100% sure if that's what you're trying to get at.

EWAN: (*Miserable.*) I'm just trying to understand.

CONNORS: I know that. Take your time.

EWAN: (*After more thought.*) Don't you think that maybe Rory is talking about vaginas and penises and big fuzzies because you and his little friends are talking about them? Maybe it's a copycat thing?

CONNORS: I see it as an empowering thing. One child finally gets up the nerve to come forward and the others take courage from that.

EWAN: You said he told you Annie put cream on his arms, and then two sessions later, he said she covered his body with peanut butter and licked it off. Well we know that Annie puts suntan lotion on them before they go outside. And I know Rory loves to embellish. Things get bigger and bigger, especially when he's got an eager audience. Don't you think it's just that? Embellishing?

CONNORS: (*After a pause.*) I think children start with a simple disclosure and then work up to the big ones when they feel safe.

EWAN: And you have no doubts?

CONNORS: Of course I have doubts. But my doubts are less important than the body of evidence accumulating.

EWAN: Last night, I lay in bed thinking. And I must admit that I conjured up one of these acts which you alluded to – between Annie Boland and my little boy. I did that. In the privacy of my own misery, in the darkness of my room. My son breathing quietly in the next room. I never thought I could do that. But I did. It was an obscene act. But I did it. I guess that's progress, is it? Are we making progress here?

CONNORS: I think that's the beginning of healing.

EWAN: I don't know how to make sense of it all, do you?

CONNORS: That's why I think counselling would be very good for your family.

EWAN: God, you're a fucking mask. You're having an intimate relationship with my four-year-old son and I can't even get a straight answer from you. Who are you?

CONNORS: I am a social worker. I work with children. I care about children.

EWAN: What do you do with all this grotesque information you collect?

CONNORS: All of the information we collect is given to the crown attorney's office, and if necessary, they lay charges.

EWAN: I don't mean that. I mean where do you put it in your head?

CONNORS: I guess one gets satisfaction out of knowing that the abuser may be punished. If we do our job well.

EWAN: I'm still not hearing a human being in there.

CONNORS: I'm not the enemy, Ewan. And I'm not under

examination here.

EWAN: Aren't you? I thought we all were. You're the expert. You hold all the cards. You're the one with all the information. You're the one with all the power.

CONNORS: I don't have any power. I have seen people do things to children which have sent me to the toilet to vomit . . . and those people are walking about today. If I had any power they wouldn't be.

EWAN: I don't deny the existence of evil in the world, and I'm sure you've seen more than your share of it, but why would a seemingly healthy, happy, nice young woman . . .

CONNORS: There is no such thing as nice! Just thousands of children living in private hells because we all want to believe in Nice . . . nobody wants to hear about it – they're too busy, too careful, too frightened of what it might mean to their carefully constructed little worlds . . . they abandon their kids. They destroy them by not listening. (*Pause, collects himself.*) We've perpetuated silence for generations . . . but it's changing now . . . the children are talking . . . and people are listening. God only knows where it's going to end. But it's been too long coming. There are a lot of wounded people scrambling to stay afloat out there, with no respect, no hope, no power. Everyone taking it out on someone smaller, weaker and it all ends up with the children.

EWAN: That's a very dark vision.

CONNORS: I guess it is. That's been my experience. Those are the pictures in my head. As for Annie Boland, she may have been abused herself as a child. That's sometimes how it happens. I don't try to understand anymore. All I try to do is ease the suffering. The suffering is real.

EWAN: (*Finally.*) Tell us what to do. We'll do anything we can to help our son through this.

ANTIGONE IN NEW YORK
by Janusc Glowacki

Serio-Comic / 2 Men
    Sasha: a Russian immigrant, homeless, 40-50
    Flea: his sometime companion, 40-50

The Setting: Thompson Square Park

Sasha and Flea have made a home out of Thompson Square Park where life can be harsh for the city's homeless. Here, they share stories of their respective homelands.

FLEA: Listen, Sasha. Listen, listen. I know you're mad at me but look. I have something for you.
(*Flea fishes a bottle with a little wine left in it out of his clothes. Tries to hand Sasha the bottle.*)
I saved it for you. Here. Take it. Some Nightrain. It's not as sweet as Cisco. Here. Take it. It's for you. I added some sterno to make it stronger. It's really good.

SASHA: No.

FLEA: (*Upset.*) What do you mean "no"? You're kidding, aren't you? What's wrong with it? It's good. Okay. It's not Wild Irish Rose but it's good. Taste it.
(*Sasha shakes his head. He takes a final look around to be sure he's gotten everything.*)

SASHA: I'm done. (*Picks up his box.*)

FLEA: Don't talk like that. You're making me nervous.
(*Tries to take the box.*)
Sasha, you can't leave like this. You are my best friend. We've had so many good times together. You want me to confess? Okay. I'll confess. I'll tell you the truth. Other people will lie to you and try to cheat you but not me. I'm not that kind of guy. You know me, right?

SASHA: I know you. Let go of my box.

FLEA: (*Takes his hands away extravagantly.*) Okay okay. I was in the boiler room last night.

SASHA: (*Sarcastic.*) Really? I can't believe it.

FLEA: Yes. And you know what else? I drank the Nightrain by myself except for this, which I saved for you.
(*Grabs the box away.*)
I won't let you go.

SASHA: Give me that back.

FLEA: (*Holds the box away from him.*) What else do you want? You want to spit in my face? Okay. Go ahead. Do it. Please. Please. Do it for me. Go ahead. Spit.

SASHA: I want a hamburger.
(*Sound of a man howling miserably from the background. Sasha grabs the bottle out of Flea's hand and drinks. Then he sits down and stretches out comfortably on the bench. Flea happily puts the box down.*)

SASHA: (*Relaxed, listens to the howling.*) You know a lot of people do that. During the day they are very docile but at night they start running around yelling, arguing, getting agitated.
(*Listens to the howl.*)
That's that Jamaican. You know, two weeks ago he pushed a twelve-year-old girl in front of a bus and she died but three days after they put him in Bellevue they let him out. They said he was too psychotic to keep.
(*The yelling continues.*)

FLEA: I think it has to do with the outdoors.

SASHA: I hear people yelling from their apartments.

FLEA: But not like they do outdoors. I think it has to do with nature. There was a guy in my village who's family was all killed by the Germans and he was very quiet and shy all day but at night he'd leave the house and you could hear him yelling from both sides of the river.

SASHA: When I lived in Leningrad. . .

FLEA: St. Petersburg.

SASHA: When I lived there it was Leningrad. I lived with my family in a big room with a kitchen. The next apartment over belonged to the KGB. They did interrogations there.

FLEA: Do you hear anything?

SASHA: Sure. People yelling.

FLEA: It was those cheap communist buildings. The walls were too thin.

SASHA: No. It was old.

FLEA: Then they had to really yell loud.

SASHA: Ja.

FLEA: Did they yell at night?

SASHA: Day and night.

FLEA: More than one shift. Well, during the day it's not so bad because people are at work.

SASHA: I was at school during the day. We had dinner at six o'clock. Whenever my father came home from work he'd turn on the radio and play loud music to drown out the yelling.

FLEA: So he liked music.

SASHA: He hated it but it was better than the yelling.

FLEA: I like yelling myself.

SASHA: My father liked paintings, especially Bosch and his Musical Hell.

FLEA: Musical Hell? What's that?

SASHA: That's what one part of Bosch's triptych was called. You know Bosch painted people crucified in hell on musical instruments: G-clefs tattooed on their asses, people upside down in drums with flutes in their assholes.

FLEA: (*Laughs.*) I like that. That's good.

SASHA: Father thought that in the 16th century Bosch had predicted our apartment in Leningrad.

FLEA: What?

SASHA: Because he used music to drown out the screaming of the condemned. That's how my father felt anyway.

FLEA: Bosch?

SASHA: Hieronymous Bosch.

FLEA: Jewish?

SASHA: No.

FLEA: Sounds Jewish.

SASHA: Ah shut up, Flea. How can you be so stupid?

FLEA: You think so?

SASHA: Absolutely. The triptych is in Madrid and my father was always dreaming about going there but they wouldn't let him so he begged his cousin in Israel to go and then write to him about it. After she went she sent him a postcard which said "I saw Bosch. He's anxious to see you and he's waiting at The Prado." Then when my father was arrested for formalism the KGB asked him how much Bosch had paid him and who his other contacts were.

FLEA: So did he turn him in?

SASHA: Flea. Flea. Fuck it. Bosch died four hundred years ago.

FLEA: Then why did he protect him?

SASHA: (*Disgusted.*) Hieronymous Bosch a Jew. He would have liked that.

FLEA: Why are you so touchy? All you Jews are like that. Jesus Christ, if I was an anti-semite would I be sitting on the same bench with you for five years? Fuckin' kike. I don't have anything against Jews.

SASHA: When I was born my mother showed me to one of our neighbors. She nodded her head and said "so tiny and already a Jew."

FLEA: You see? People are sympathetic. Was she Polish?

SASHA: No. Russian.

FLEA: You know during the war a few Jews in our village were denounced to the Nazis. But mostly they were the ones who'd escaped from the trains and were all busted up anyway. Then it turned out there was a man in our village named Masiak Antoni who, without telling anyone, hid a Jew in his barn. No one found out. And then, when the war was over, the Jew came out and went to Israel. Then he started sending Masiak packages and money. Masiak was practically drowning in the stuff this guy sent him. Unbelievable. Masiak bought a car and every Sunday you could see him driving to Church wearing a permanent press shirt. And his wife and two daughters all had nylons on and the people who had denounced Jews watched them go by and cried and beat their heads against the trees. And since then, let me tell you, no Jew will ever be denounced in Poland again. At least not in my village.

(*During his speech Sasha lies down and tries to sleep. On the next bench Flea does the same.*)

AVEN'U BOYS
by Frank Pugliese

Serio-Comic / 3 Men
   Rocky, Ed and Charlie: three Bensonhurst teenagers, crude,
      racist and violent

The Setting: Bensonhurst, Brooklyn

Driven by hatred and ignorance, these three friends here display
their penchant for homophobia.

O   O   O

(*Lights up on the boys. This time, the action of the scene is
that each boy is trying to stick a finger up the other boy's
buttocks or slap them with a limp backhand to the groin. If
they success in the groin, they say "duck." In the buttocks,
they say "goose." It is a game they often play. Charlie has a
bag with an open wine bottle in it that they pass around.*)

ED: Don't be drinking that poison.

CHARLIE: What?

ED: Wine ain't supposed to fizz.

CHARLIE: It's apple wine. Doctor's away and shit.

ED: It'll burn little holes in your stomach. They put in anti-freeze.
   (*Ed ducks Charlie.*)

CHARLIE: Where the fuck is wine gonna freeze?

ED: Stick it in the freezer. It don't freeze. My uncle puts it in his
   radiator.
   (*He gooses Charlie.*)

ROCKY: Science, I tell ya.

CHARLIE: Maybe that's why I throw up every morning.

ROCKY: Hey Ed, sweetie. Heard you took a honeymoon with a
   faggot-ass.
   (*He gooses Ed.*)

ED: Bullshit.

ROCKY: That's the word.

ED: Who said it? Who? I'll break his fuckin' legs!
   (*Ed ducks Rocky.*)

ROCKY: Word is they did you in the bar under the bridge . . . Ain't that the word, Charlie?

(*He gooses Charlie.*)

CHARLIE: Fuck up man.

(*He ducks Rocky, who then gooses him. They start bouncing around and trying to smack each other.*)

ED: Boys. Boys.

(*They don't stop.*)

Cut the shit!

(*They stop.*)

It was nothin'.

CHARLIE: We were flyin'. We were celebratin', the guy died a retard. He never fingered us. . .

ED: So now you can shut up about it already.

CHARLIE: Ed, didn't them fuckin' girls look beautiful? Didn't they?

ED: I coulda sworn they was girls.

CHARLIE: You shoulda seen them swayin' and bumpin' their round asses all over the dance floor.

ED: It was blonde night. You got free drinks if you was blonde. Blondes all over. I love blondes.

CHARLIE: And what a blonde. She had tits out to here. I mean he had tits. Shit I mean he looked like he had tits. It had tits out to here. I'm confused.

ED: She was gorgeous.

(*He ducks Rocky.*)

CHARLIE: Even if she was a guy, I swear.

(*Ed ducks him. He doubles over.*)

ED: She was definitely the best looking out there.

ROCKY: She was a he?

CHARLIE: She was real sexy. She goes to Ed, "Why don't you come out with me?"

ED: I figured I'm gonna score with a woman. Not some girl.

CHARLIE: She was all over him. They were makin' out on the dance floor like newlyweds. Show him the hickey, Ed.

ED: Shut up Charlie. Shut the fuck up. You know, you don't know when to keep that dumb-ass mouth shut. One day I'm gonna knock it off your face. Now shut up. That stuff ain't important.

ROCKY: So when you fuck the faggot ass?

ED: I didn't . . . I just go out when she, he grabs me in the alley. And starts playing the skin flute. I didn't know what's happenin'.

CHARLIE: That's when I came out and I saw her goin' on him like a locomotive. Chug a chug. She was flyin' up and down, up and down.

ED: Shut up. Who's tellin' this story, you or me?

CHARLIE: You.

ED: So why you gotta open your mouth all the time. If I'm tellin' the story, let me tell the story.

CHARLIE: Alright, tell the story. Just you ain't tellin' it right.

ED: Look if I want you to tell it, I'll tell ya.

ROCKY: So when you fuck him?

ED: I didn't fuck no faggot . . . Now I see her flyin' on me up and down. I mean, no girl's gonna do what she likes. Like the man is gotta be in control. Right?

ROCKY: Right.

ED: Right Charlie?

CHARLIE: Oh, so I can talk now?

ED: Yeah.

CHARLIE: Right, Ed.

ED: So I decide to give her what she wants. I'm gonna fuck her brains out. So I reach for her snatch. . .

CHARLIE: That's when this tremendous dick flies out. And guess what, it wasn't Ed's.

ED: Charlie you're pissin' me off.
(*He ducks Charlie hard.*)
Shut up.

ROCKY: Sounds like the story goin' 'round. Ed the fag-fucker.

ED: Shut your mouth . . . So I see this tremendous dick fly out, and it wasn't mine. I was pissed off, so I called Charlie over and we kicked the shit out of him. . .

CHARLIE: I held him down and Ed jammed a bottle up his ass.
(*Ed stares at Charlie and then ducks him.*)
I'm just finishing the story.

ED: Charlie held him down. But I was just teachin' a lesson that's all. Fuckin' no good dirty AIDS-ass-faggot.

CHARLIE: Ed was like an animal.

ED: (*Smacks Charlie.*) Shut up! I was just teachin' him a lesson.

ROCKY: Well Ed, the whole school's thinkin' maybe you like to give it up the ass . . . Maybe you is the fag.

ED: Who said that? I'll kill them.

ROCKY: But don't worry Ed, all the great artists were butt-fuckers. Hey Ed, maybe you're a great artist. (*He gooses Ed.*)

CHARLIE: Yeah, a bullshit artist.

ED: You better tell me who's spreadin' that story or I'm gonna twist your peckers off.

(*Charlie gooses Ed and Rocky ducks him.*)

ROCKY: What if it's true, Ed, one mornin' you'll wake up and just all of a sudden wanna suck cock.

CHARLIE: You'll start wearing funny girl clothes.

(*Charlie gooses Ed.*)

ED: I ain't laughin'.

CHARLIE: Yeah and you'll be in the Village wearing leather, playin' with little boys and walkin' poodles . . . Maybe it's some disease you caught from the blonde.

(*Ed puts him in a headlock.*)

ED: I'll kill you.

ROCKY: Shit Ed, huggin' boys already? I see it comin'.

ED: Charlie grab him or I'll kill you.

CHARLIE: We's only kiddin'.

ROCKY: Whatta you gonna do to me, butt-fuck me?

ED: Charlie grab him. (*Grabs the bottle.*) Who told you?

CHARLIE: How's Rocky gonna know?

(*He grabs Rocky and covers his mouth. Rocky mumbles.*)

ROCKY: Hey let go. I'll kill you, you faggot. Let go.

ED: Shut up.

(*He pulls down Rocky's pants and is ready to jam the bottle.*)

ROCKY: CHARLIE. CHARLIE'S TELLIN' EVERYBODY YOU FUCKED A FAGGOT.

CHARLIE: SHUT UP!

(*Ed lets go of Rocky.*)

He's lyin'.

ED: I'm so fuckin' stupid.

(*Charlie runs away.*)

And don't come back.

CONVERSATIONS WITH MY FATHER
by Herb Gardner

Serio-Comic / 2 Men
   Eddie: a Russian Jew determined to make it in America,
     20-30
   Joey: his 10-year-old son

The Setting: a tavern on Canal Street, New York City, 1936

Eddie has escaped the Cossacks and made a new life for his family in New York, where they own and operate a tavern. When young Joey is harassed by another boy in the neighborhood, Eddie offers some pointers in the fine art of fisticuffs.

O   O   O

JOEY: (*Entering, thoughtfully, with stack of mail.*) Pop, the sign outside, it says "Ross" on it . . .

EDDIE: That's our new name, you're gonna love it; honor o'Barney himself. (*Takes mail, starts going through it.*)

JOEY: You mean not just for the place, but actually our new name?

EDDIE: All done; legit and legal, kid. Al Gladstone presidin' – (*Takes envelope from mail.*) Son of a bitch, The Sons of Moses, Pop's *yahrzeit* again. . .

JOEY: So my name is Joe Ross? That's my name now? Joe Ross? Very . . . brief, that name . . .

EDDIE: (*Studying blue card from envelope.*) Fifteen *years*, they find me every time, it's the Royal Mounted Rabbis . . .

JOEY: Joe Ross, it starts – it's over . . .

EDDIE: Hey, *Hebrew* School -

JOEY: (*Suddenly alarmed.*) Jeez, went right outa my *mind* – (*Grabs Hebrew-texts, races for door, slapping yarmulkeh on his head.*)

EDDIE: *Wait* a minute – (*Points to yarmulkeh.*) Where ya goin' with *that* on your head? What're ya, crazy? Ya gonna go eight blocks through Little Italy and Irishtown, passin' right through Goddamn *Polack* Street, with *that* on your head? How many times I gotta tell ya, kid – that is *not* an outdoor garment. That is an indoor garment *only*. Why don't ya wear a sign on your head says, "Please come kick the shit outa me?" You put it on in Hebrew School, where it belongs.

JOEY: Pop, I don't –

EDDIE: I'm tellin' ya *once* more – stow the yammy, kid. *Stow* it.

JOEY: (*Whips yarmulkeh off, shoves it in a pocket.*) O.K., O.K. (*Starts toward door.*) I just don't see why I gotta be ashamed.

EDDIE: I'm not askin' ya to be ashamed. I'm askin' ya to be smart. (*Sees something in the mail as Joey opens door; sharply.*) Hold it –

JOEY: Gotta go, Pop –

EDDIE: Hold it right it there –

JOEY: Pop, this Tannenbaum, he's a killer –

EDDIE: (*Looking down at mail, solemnly.*) I got information here says you ain't *seein'* Tannenbaum this morning. I got information here says you ain't even headed for Hebrew School right now. (*Silence for a moment. Joey remains in doorway.*) C'mere, we gotta talk.

JOEY: (*Approaching cautiously, keeping at a safe distance.*) Hey . . . no whackin', Pop . . .

EDDIE: I got this note here; says – (*Takes small piece of cardboard from mail, reads.*) "Dear Sheenie Bastard. Back of Carmine's, Remind you, Jewshit Joe, Eight o'clock A.M., Be there. Going to make Hamburger out of Goldberger – S.D." Bastard is spelled here B-A-S-T-I-D; this and the humorous remarks I figure the fine mind of the wop, DeSapio. (*After a moment, looks up, slaps bar.*) And I wanna tell ya *good* luck, *glad* you're goin', you're gonna *nail* 'im, you're gonna *finish* 'im, you're gonna murder 'im.

JOEY: Wait a minute – it's O.K.? Really?

EDDIE: – and here's a couple pointers how to do so.

JOEY: Pointers? *Pointers*? – I need a *shot*-gun, Pop; DeSapio's near twice my size, fourteen years *old* –

EDDIE: Hey, far *be* it! Far be it from me to give pointers – a guy got twenty six bouts under his belt, *twelve* professional –

JOEY: Yeah, but this DeSapio, he really *hates* me, this kid; he hated me the minute he *saw* me. He says we killed Christ, us Jews.

EDDIE: They was *all* Jews there, kid, everybody; Christ, His mother, His whole crowd – you tell him there was a buncha Romans there too, makes him *directly related* to the guys done the actual hit!

JOEY: I *told* him that Pop – that's when he *whacked* me.

EDDIE: And I bet you whacked him back, which is appropriate; *no* shit from *no*body, ya stuck to your *guns*, kid –

JOEY: So why're we hidin' then? How come we're "Ross" all of a sudden? (*With an edge.*) Or maybe Ross is just our outdoor name, and Goldberg's still our indoor name.

EDDIE: *Hey* –

JOEY: I don't *get* it, this mean we're not Jewish anymore?

EDDIE: Of *course* we're still Jewish; we're just not gonna *push* it.

JOEY: (*Checking watch.*) Jeez – three minutes to eight, Pop, takes five to get there, he's gonna think I'm chicken – (*Starts toward door.*)

EDDIE: *One* minute for two pointers; let 'em wait, he'll get anxious –

JOEY: He's *not anxious*, Pop, I promise ya –

EDDIE: Now, these pointers is based on my observations o' your natural talents; the bounce,the eye, the smarts –

JOEY: (*Protesting.*) *Pop* –

EDDIE: C'mon, I seen you take out Itchy Halloran with one shot in fronta the Texaco Station; who're we *kiddin'* here? Hey, I was O.K., but *you* got potential I *never* had.

JOEY: But Itchy Halloran's *my height*, DeSapio's twice my *size* –

EDDIE: (*Ignoring him.*) O.K., first blow; your instinct is go for the belly, right?

JOEY: *Instinct*? His belly is as high as I can *reach*, Pop –

EDDIE: Wrong: first blow, forget the belly. Pointer Number One – ya listenin'?

JOEY: Yeah.

EDDIE: (*Demonstrating, precisely.*) Considerin' the size, you gotta rock this boy *early* . . . gotta take the first one up from the *ground, vertical*, so your full body-weight's in the shot. Now, start of the fight, right away, *imm*ediate, you hunk *down*, move outa range; then *he's* gotta come to *you* – and you meet him with a right fist up *off the ground*; picture a spot in the middle of his chin and aim for it – (*Demonstrates blow, Joey copies.*) then comes the important part –

JOEY: What's that?

EDDIE: Jump back.

JOEY: Jump back?

EDDIE: Yeah, ya jump back so when he falls he don't hurt ya.

JOEY: When he *falls*? *Murder*, he's gonna murder me. Pop, Pop, this is an *execution* I'm goin' to here! I'm only goin' so I won't be ashamed!

EDDIE: There's only one thing you gotta watch out for –

JOEY: *Death*, I gotta watch out for *death* –

EDDIE: Not death . . . but there could be some damage. Could turn out to be more than one guy there, you're gettin' ganged up on, somethin' *special* – this *happens*, kid – O.K., we got a weapon here – (*Takes framed photo of boxer from wall.*) we got a weapon here, guaranteed. (*Hands photo to Joey.*) What's it say there?

JOEY: (*Reading.*) "Anybody gives *you* trouble, give *me* trouble. I love you. Love, Vince."

EDDIE: O.K.; June Four, Nineteen Twenty-one, I come into the ring against Vince DiGangi, they bill him "The Ghetto Gorilla," – a shrimp with a moustache, nothin', I figure an easy win. Five *seconds* into Round One comes a *chamalia* from this little Eye-tie – I'm out, I'm on the canvas, your Pop is *furniture*, Joey. I open one eye, *there's* DiGangi on his knees next to me, he's got me in his arms, he's huggin' me, he's kissin' my face, he loves me. I give him his first big win, his first knockout. I *made* him, he says, he's gonna love me forever. And he *does*. That's the nice thing about these Telanas, they love ya or they hate ya, but it's forever; *so, remember* – (*Leans towards him.*) things get outa hand, you got a group situation, somethin' – you holler "DiGangi é mio fratello, *chiamalo*!" (*Grips his shoulder.*) "DiGangi é mio fratello, *chiamalo*!" Say it.

JOEY: "DiGangi é mio fratello, chi . . . amalo!"

EDDIE: That's: "DiGangi's my brother, *call* him!" (*Softly, awe-struck, imitating their response.*) Whoa . . . "DiGangi" 's the magic word down there, biggest hit since Columbus, lotta power with the mob. Perhaps you noticed, Big Vito don't come around here pushin' protection, whatever. This is the result of *one* word from Mr. Vincent DiGangi. (*Pats Joey's hand.*) Very heavy ticket there, kid, you don't want to use it unless the straits is completely dire. (*Slaps bar.*) O.K., ya got all that?

JOEY: (*Starting towards front door without much spirit.*) Yeah. (*As he passes stroller; softly, sighing.*) Well . . . here I go, Charlie.

THE DESTINY OF ME
by Larry Kramer

Dramatic / 2 Men
> Ned and Ben: brothers coming to terms with their lives and
> their deaths, 40-50

The Setting: autumn, 1992, outside Washington, D.C.

After many years of battling social ignorance and political
treachery, Ned, an HIV-positive activist, has allowed himself to
participate in an experimental procedure that promises a cure.
His older brother, Ben, visits him in the hospital, and they discuss
the past and the future.

○　　　○　　　○

NED: (*Screaming out.*) Ben!

BEN: (*Lying on a cot next to him.*) I'm here, Ned.

NED: Ben?

BEN: Yes, Ned.

NED: I'm scared.

BEN: It's alright. Go to sleep.

NED: Ben, I love you.

BEN: I love you, too.

NED: I can't say it enough. It's funny, but life is very precious
now.

BEN: Why's it funny? I understand, and it is for me, too. A
colleague of mine with terminal cancer went into his
bathroom last week and blew his brains out with a shotgun.
(*Dawn is breaking outside. Ben gets up. He throws some cold
water on his face at the sink.*)

NED: Hey, cheer me up, Lemon.

BEN: They haven't struck us out yet.

NED: What if this doesn't work?

BEN: It's going to work (*Sits beside him on bed.*)

NED: Even if it does, it will only work for a while.

BEN: Then we'll worry about it in a while.

NED: You've certainly spent a great deal of your life trying to keep me alive, and I've been so much trouble, always trying to kill myself, asking your advice on every breath I take, putting you to the test endlessly.

BEN: I beat you up once.

NED: You beat me up? When?

BEN: We were kids. I was trying to teach you how to tackle in football. You were fast, quick. I thought you could be a quarterback. And you wouldn't do it right. You didn't want to learn. It was just perversity on your part. So I decided to teach you a lesson. I blocked you and blocked you, as hard as I could, much harder than I had to. And then I tackled you, and you'd get up and I'd tackle you again, harder. You just kept getting up for more. I beat you up real bad.

NED: I don't remember any of that. Now why did you go and do all that?

BEN: A thousand reasons and who knows?

NED: I don't want to be cremated, I want to be buried, with a tombstone, so people can come and visit and find me. Do you want to be buried or cremated?

BEN: Neither.

NED: What will they do with you?

BEN: I don't care.

NED: How can you not care?

BEN: I won't be here.

NED: You don't want people to remember you?

BEN: I've never thought about it.

NED: It seems like I've spent my whole life thinking about it. How can you never have thought about it?

BEN: I never thought about it.

NED: Well, think about it.

BEN: I don't want to think about it.

NED: I just thought we could be buried side by side.

BEN: Please, Ned. You're not go –

NED: I've picked out the cemetery. It's a pretty place. George Balanchine is buried there. I danced around his grave. When no once could see me.

BEN: Are we finished with the morbid part of this conversation?

NED: No. I want my name on something. A building. At Yale, for gay students, or in New York. Will you look after that for me?

BEN: You'll have many years to arrange all that yourself.

NED: But you're my lawyer!

BEN: Everything will be taken care of.

NED: Then the rest of my money, you give to the kids and Sara, please give something special to Sara. You married her and you didn't even love her. And you grew to love her. I'm sorry I never really had that. For very long.

BEN: I want you to know . . . I want you to know . . . I'm proud you've stood up for what you've believed in. I've even been a little jealous of all the attention you've received. I think to myself that if I'd gone off on my own instead of building the firm, I could have taken up some cause and done it better than you. But I didn't do that and you have and I admire you for that.

NED: I guess you could have lived without me. I never could have lived without you. Go back to your hotel.

BEN: I'll see you tomorrow.

THE DOLPHIN POSITION
by Percy Granger

Serio-Comic / 2 Men
> Jerry: a stressed-out ad man, 30-40
> Paul: his ex-partner, 40-50

The Setting: here and now

Jerry has awakened to find his life turned upside down. His wife and son – who he seems to have forgotten completely – have left him to move to Vermont. Here, a very confused Jerry goes to his ex-partner for help.

JERRY: What is Vermont? Trees? Mountains? I need visuals. Paul's my art director, he'll help me. Paul? Paul?
(*He turns the dial. Paul appears in a tu-tu and cardigan sweater over his slacks as the lights change to a green mottled hue and forest sounds are heard.*)
What the hell is this?

PAUL: (*Referring to the costume.*) I could ask you the same question.

JERRY: (*Whips the costume off.*) Get serious, man, we got work to do.

PAUL: I don't work anymore, Jerry. I'm retired.

JERRY: Well, you're going to work now because this is all your fault.

PAUL: What is?

JERRY: Why didn't you tell me I was married?

PAUL: Would it have made any difference?

JERRY: It might have.

PAUL: Jerry, Jerry, Jerry, aren't you the person who told me that God invented women because he couldn't teach sheep how to cook?

JERRY: No!

PAUL: Here, you'd better take this.
(*He holds out his empty hand.*)

JERRY: What is it?

PAUL: A fishing pole.

JERRY: Fishing –?

PAUL: (*He sits on the living room totem.*) This is a great spot. They've been biting like crazy all week.

(*He casts an imaginary line. Jerry becomes aware of the forest sounds.*)

JERRY: Paul, are you in my mind?

PAUL: I'm on your mind.

JERRY: Is this real?

PAUL: I don't know . . . but I love the question. Want a beer? (*He pops Jerry an imaginary beer and pops one for himself.*)

JERRY: Paul, I want my –

PAUL: – wife back, I know.

JERRY: And my son.

PAUL: Jerry, relax, drink your beer . . . Sit down and let me ask you something. Did your wife ever, by any chance, call you an emotional void?

JERRY: Yes – but I deserved it.

PAUL: (*Chuckling.*) What a chump.

JERRY: A chump?

PAUL: That's what women *want* us to think. They've buffaloed us into believing that the sensitivity shortfall's all our fault. *But* did you ever try opening up to her?

JERRY: Yes.

PAUL: And what happened?

JERRY: She left me.

PAUL: Bingo! You see? Either they jump all over you for saying what's really on your mind or they dump you for a wimp.

JERRY: Paul, how is this getting us to Vermont?

PAUL: It's not. St. Paul was right two thousand years ago; men and women have nothing in common.

JERRY: That can't be right, can it?

PAUL: The truce held so long as women know their place. But once they went over the top screaming, "I want it all!" they were fair game. Do we have it all? Do you?

JERRY: Well, no.

PAUL: Of course not. We're in harness all day long while they sit home watching Phil Donahue tell' em about the perfect relationship. Do we have time to think about the perfect relationship?

JERRY: Maybe we should.

PAUL: Our fantasies gotta be quick. Get 'em taken care of and get back on the line. We have heart attacks, what do they have? Of course they win all the arguments, they start' em. The minute we leave for the office, they pick the high ground and spend the whole day digging in. We come home fried, we haven't read the latest Cosmo questionnaire on "Why Does Your Marriage Suck?" We don't know our asses from a lug wrench! We're in a state of innocence. And what do they do? They hammer us!

JERRY: Hey Paul, slow down. What's wrong? Aren't there any pharmacists in Maine?

PAUL: You got a bite.

JERRY: What?

PAUL: Reel it in, reel it in.

(*He takes Jerry's line and reels it in. He grabs the wiggling fish.*)

She's a beauty, isn't she? We're gonna feast tonight, pal. It doesn't get any better than this.

JERRY: Paul, there's nothing there.

PAUL: "You want me to take you out for sushi, honey? I got your fucking sushi right here."

(*He takes a bite of the fish.*)

JERRY: Paul, I can hear my own voice.

PAUL: Because it's you talking, man. It's not me. I'm just telling you what you know.

JERRY: That's what got me into trouble. I want to find out what I don't know. What does this guy Todd have that I don't?

PAUL: Jerry, you're confusing love with the competitive instinct.

JERRY: Come on, I want the enchanted sword.

PAUL: (*Sighs.*) Okay. He talks to her.

JERRY: And?

PAUL: He listens.

JERRY: And?

PAUL: That's it.

JERRY: That's it?

PAUL: That's all women want, Jerry. They don't want money or power or even, God forbid, sex. All women want, Mr. Freud, is our undivided attention. You give any woman that and she'll fall in love with you. They're completely unselective.

(*Jerry rises and drags Paul to his feet.*)

JERRY: Get vertical, man.

PAUL: Come back to the locker room, Jerry –

JERRY: No!

PAUL: All right, all right, you pass the third test. What's the concept?

JERRY: Vermont.

PAUL: Vermont's a big place.

JERRY: If we can't make Vermont be what we want it to be, we don't deserve to live.

EARL, OLLIE, AUSTIN & RALPH
by Glenn Rawles

Serio-Comic / 2 Men
Earl and Ollie: longtime lovers and hotel owners, 70s

The Setting: the Blue Angel Hotel, Myrtle Beach, the present

Here, Earl and Ollie trade affectionate barbs and memories while sitting on the front porch of their old hotel.

OLLIE: Why'd you tell Rogers we weren't going for a walk tonight? We always walk. The kids are fine.

EARL: Cause when Rogers goes with us, he spends all his time looking for "lost" things on the ground trying to look up boys' gym shorts.

OLLIE: Sometimes he finds something. (*Smiles.*) Then we help. Taking us out for dinner, did he say?

EARL: Yeah, before he leaves.

OLLIE: Isn't that nice.

EARL: It is.

OLLIE: Not like him.

EARL: No. I told him he was a whore.

OLLIE: He find the redhead?

EARL: Like a hound on a fox.

OLLIE: The man has radar.

EARL: He was talking about the time the blond boy got naked and hung off our neon sign.

OLLIE: The big guy.

EARL: Yeah.

OLLIE: He was brunette.

EARL: No, blond, he had white-blond hair.

OLLIE: Not everywhere he didn't.

EARL: Not a blond.

OLLIE: Never. I told you that.

EARL: No.

OLLIE: Yeah.

EARL: Did you?

OLLIE: Sure.

EARL: Hm. Thought he was a blond.

OLLIE: He was big, though.

EARL: No kidding, how'd he walk?

OLLIE: Almost didn't need a ladder to get down.

(*They laugh.*)

EARL: Pretty funny.

OLLIE: Pretty funny.

EARL: You know –

OLLIE: Yeah?

EARL: Talking to Rogers –

OLLIE: Yeah?

EARL: We've always called him Rogers.

OLLIE: Fifty years.

EARL: But it's Mr. Rogers.

OLLIE: Right, we call him by his last name.

EARL: What's his first name?

OLLIE: Oh, don't be stupid.

EARL: I can't remember.

OLLIE: (*Smacks his lips in disgust.*) Shew.

EARL: Okay, so perfect, you tell me.

OLLIE: (*Doesn't remember.*) Um – it's – um – uh – Richard. Richard.

EARL: Richard, Richard. Richard Rogers. No. No, no, Richard Rogers, he's a musician. Wrote songs.

OLLIE: Lyrics.

EARL: Songs.

OLLIE: Lyrics.

EARL: You're still wrong, it's not Richard.

OLLIE: So, who cares? As long as he doesn't know we don't know, who knows? I mean we call him by his last name, and as long as we don't forget –

EARL: Right. As long as we remember.

OLLIE: Absolutely. We can write it down on the register, so we won't forget.

EARL: To forget is human – no, to forget is divine.

OLLIE: No, FORGIVE is divine, forget is – well, forget doesn't have a proverb. As long as we don't forget.

EARL: Forget what?

OLLIE: Forget whatever we were talking about, doo-doo brain. Schmuck-head.

EARL: Which was?

OLLIE: What?

EARL: Aha! You forgot too.

OLLIE: For your information, we were talking about "Oklahoma." And "South Pacific."

EARL: Well, alright, I'll give you that one.

OLLIE: I have a question.

EARL: (*He picks up magazine.*) Is this the new "National Geographic"?

OLLIE: Yes. Now, here's my question:

EARL: See the new space pictures?

OLLIE: You're not listening, you're not paying me a bit of attention, I'm asking a question, and it involves what we were talking about before.

EARL: Oklahoma?

OLLIE: No, before Oklahoma, about the boy.

EARL: Boy?

OLLIE: The not-blond boy with the big that hung off our neon sign?

EARL: I remember.

OLLIE: It is my understanding that when women get older, their titties sag, often, say, down to their knees.

EARL: How would you know?

OLLIE: Well, you're holding the "National Geographic," you tell me. I said it was my "understanding," don't get jealous.

EARL: I thought we were talking about Mr. Rogers before.

OLLIE: Mr. Rogers? On TV?

EARL: No, Jasper Rogers, we've known him for fifty years, he's taking us out to the fish camp before he leaves.

OLLIE: That's nice.

EARL: Yeah.

OLLIE: Not like him.

EARL: No.

OLLIE: Anyway, my question is this: if, as is my understanding, women's titties sag to their knees when they're our age, why don't our whackers sag to our knees? I mean, a sight like that could really get some respect out of those pushy teen types.

EARL: You wouldn't want it down to your knees.

OLLIE: Speak for yourself.

EARL: No, I mean, think of all the blood it would take to make it rise back up. It'd suck all the blood out of your body. Your head would collapse into your neck.

OLLIE: Let's write "National Geographic" and ask them.

EARL: Wait a minute. Here's a subscription card.

OLLIE: Got postage on the back?

EARL: Yep.

OLLIE: Well, scratch through all their crap and write our question.

EARL: (*Takes pen from pocket, writes.*)
If – wo-men's – tit – ties — sag – to – their – knees – why – don't – men's – whackers . . .

OLLIE: Well, don't say whackers, say "penises."

EARL: Too late. (*He laughs.*)

OLLIE: (*Laughs.*) I wonder if the "National Geographic" will know what a whacker is?

EARL: I don't think so, I've looked for pictures of *them* for years.

OLLIE: They're awfully prejudiced. (*They laugh.*)

EARL: Gonna mail it?

OLLIE: Nah.

EARL: Mail it.

OLLIE: Nah.

EARL: What the hell.

OLLIE: What the hell.
(*Ollie gets up and goes inside to the desk, drops it through the slot, and goes back to the porch.*)
It's government property now, too late.

EARL: Good.
(*They chuckle.*)
What is it? Something's in the air tonight?

OLLIE: Nice night. No, I feel it too. Something –

EARL: Yeah. Something.

OLLIE: Something good.

EARL: I love you, Ollie.

OLLIE: I love you, Earl. (*They hold hands, pause.*)
It's been a nice fifty years.

EARL: It's fair.
(*A pause. Earl laughs, Ollie playfully slaps Earl's hand.*)

OLLIE: Geekhead from hell.
(*Lights out.*)

THE ICE FISHING PLAY
by Kevin Kling

Serio-Comic / 3 Men
> Ron: an ice fisherman
> Brother Francis & Brother Shumway: 2 wandering
>   missionaries, 20-30

The Setting: an ice fishing house on a lake in northern Minnesota

In the privacy of his ice house, Ben is free to contemplate his life. His solitude is interrupted when two missionaries invade the ice house in hopes of saving his soul.

O   O   O

(*Ron answers the door, The wind is blowing.*)
FRANCIS: Good day, brother.
RON: Hey.
FRANCIS: My name is Brother Francis and this is Brother Shumway.
(*There is a loud sneeze.*)
RON: Bless you.
SHUMWAY'S VOICE: Thank you.
FRANCIS: Could we trouble you for a minute of your time?
RON: Well . . .
FRANCIS: Please, brother it's a matter of the utmost importance. Life and death . . .
RON: Well, yeah, come on in.
(*Brothers Francis and Shumway enter. They have red faces and cotton snow on their shoulders. During the next dialogue Francis takes the towel, wipes off the red and takes off the snow and puts it near Ron's. Shumway wipes his face but the red won't come off, likewise the snow is sewn on his jacket and hat.*)
FRANCIS: The Grand Climax is at hand.
RON: Oh, you don't say. Now which grand climax is that?
FRANCIS: Brother, would you read this passage? Please?

(Francis shows Ron a passage in a book.)

RON: Happy is he who reads aloud and those who hear the words of prophecy, and who observe the things written in it: for the appointed time is near.

FRANCIS: Revelation 1:3. Can you tell me what that means?

RON: I gotta admit I don't have a clue.

FRANCIS: Because your soul is not at rest, ready to comprehend the words of the Lord.

RON: No, I don't know because when I read aloud I gotta concentrate on the words, not their meaning, so I can't tell you what it means. Now if you were to let me read it to myself I don't have to worry about all that.

(Francis holds out the book, Ron reads to himself.)

Well apparently you're happy when it's time for your appointment?

FRANCIS: Good. Right. You're happy about an appointment. Now. Brother, do you know who this is?

(Shows Ron a photo in a book.)

RON: Yeah . . . Oh, who is that. It's uh, it's oh shit . . . it's right on the tip of my tongue . . . Godammit who is that . . . Christ, I outta know . . .

FRANCIS: It's Moses.

RON: No that's not it. I know, it's Charlton Heston, that's who it is. Bird Man of Alcatraz.

FRANCIS: No.

SHUMWAY: That's Burt Lancaster.

FRANCIS: It's Moses.

SHUMWAY: I mean who played Bird Man of Alcatraz.

RON: No, Burt Lancaster you're thinking of Barabbass.

SHUMWAY: That's Anthony Quinn.

RON: No, he's Spartacus.

SHUMWAY: Nope, Kirk Douglas.

RON: He's Sampson.

FRANCIS: It's Moses.

SHUMWAY: No, that's Victor Mature.

RON: No, Victor Mature, that's Hercules.

SHUMWAY: Joe Bonamo was Hercules.

RON: I'll be, that was Joe Bonamo. Then the Bird Man of Alcatraz was Burt Lancaster. But this here, that's Charlton Heston.

SHUMWAY: Right.

FRANCIS: IT'S MOSES. Moses. Moses.

(*Francis glares at Shumway. Shumway sneezes.*)

RON: Bless you.

SHUMWAY: Thank you.

FRANCIS: Alright, now brother, this time look carefully. Do you know who this is?

RON: Oh yeah, that's easy. That would be Willem Def . . .

FRANCIS: NO!

RON: Alright but I seen that one twice.

FRANCIS: Jesus, it's Jesus. Lord of lords, King of kings Jesus. You've heard of Jesus?

RON: Of course I have but you asked me who he was not who he was playing.

FRANCIS: This is the real Jesus. Those are characters in movies. Not real. Movies. Particles of light. Written by people, not God. You can't trust anything written by people. Human interpretations and publications are fallible. Like Joseph of old would say . . .

SHUMWAY: Do not interpretations belong to God?

FRANCIS: Shumway, please.

SHUMWAY: Genesis 40:8

FRANCIS: SHUMWAY. And please blow your nose. There are twenty six letters in our Lord's alphabet not twenty four. (*Back to Ron.*) Brother, I happened to notice you enjoy the fine art of fishing.

RON: Does the Pope . . . I mean, is a nun's . . . Yeah.

FRANCIS: Did you know that Jesus was also a fisherman?

RON: It only makes sense.

FRANCIS: And do you also recall the parable of the loaves and fishes where Jesus fed five thousand people on two fish . . .

RON: (*To Shumway.*) I'd give fifty bucks to see the Game Warden's face when he heard that one.

(*Ron and Shumway crack up.*)

FRANCIS: Shumway, would you please wait for me outside?

SHUMWAY: Outside?

FRANCIS: Yes, until we're through here, please.

SHUMWAY: No.

FRANCIS: No?

SHUMWAY: No I . . . I have a prayer.

FRANCIS: Very well, brother Shumway, you may lead us in a closing prayer. (*Francis loudly clears his throat.*)

SHUMWAY: God, I don't understand. I know as God you cannot be understood except by yourself. So if we are to understand you we can only do so by being transformed into you, so that we know you as you know yourself. And since we will not know you as you know yourself until we are united into what you are. Faith seems to play a large role in this and . . . I . . . I don't know if . . . if I . . .

(*Shumway breaks down.*)

FRANCIS: It's alright, brother. In His name we pray.

SHUMWAY: Amen.

FRANCIS: Thank you, Brother. Now wait for me outside. I'll only be a moment.

(*Shumway nods and exits.*)

I don't think he's going to make it.

RON: Me neither.

FRANCIS: He doesn't have what it takes.

RON: Like a coat.

FRANCIS: Brother, am I not subjected to the same infirmities? Yet here I stand strong and solid in my beliefs. Brother Shumway is weak because he has doubts. Be that as it may, I will not quit his mission and soon he will be welcomed into the arms of our Lord. I can guarantee Brother Shumway will have solace. Can you say the same? The apocalypse is near, there will be a judgment.

RON: It sounds more to me like the end of your bible is near. Now go on and get out there, you nut, and bring your buddy back in here till the storm is passed.

(*Francis starts to exit. Stops.*)

FRANCIS: Brother Ron, I know why you are out here on this pristine lake void of life, this sanctuary.

RON: You do, huh?

FRANCIS: Yes. But you cannot escape, brother, for the devil you fear is not searching without, it lives within. The Lord sayeth the more we are alone the more we are together. Remember that brother. One day death will knock upon that door . . . and on that day Brother Ron, may your debts be paid in full and peace be yours. Good day.

(*Francis exits. The wind is blowing.*)

RON: WERE YOU BORN IN A BARN?

AN IMAGINARY LIFE
by Peter Parnell

Serio-Comic / 2 Men
   Matt: a semi-professional playwright, 40s
   Igor: a Polish immigrant struggling to become a playwright,
      30s

The Setting: an apartment in New York, the present

In an impulsive moment, Matt promised to help Igor with his play. When the intense Pole shows up in Matt's apartment, it becomes obvious that Matt bit off more than he was prepared to chew.

O   O   O

IGOR: This is some swell place you have here, Mr. Ableman.

MATT: Thanks. Uh – why don't we run down to the nearest coffee shop?

IGOR: Coffee shop? No. I never eat the food in such places!

MATT: I only thought, if you hadn't had breakfast . . .

IGOR: No, I am fine . . . An early riser. I will leave this and go. But first I must tell you, I am a great admirer of your work. A fan. I saw your last play when it was presented Off-Broadway at the Hinterlands Theatre Company.

MATT: You saw that?

IGOR: Many times, sir. You were on a double bill with that other wonderful writer. The one who won this year's Nobel Prize . . .

MATT: Oh . . . Yes . . .

IGOR: Spencer Glick.

MATT: It was the Pulitzer, not the Nobel, Igor. The Nobel comes *next* year.

IGOR: He has been having a good year, hasn't he?

MATT: A good year? How about a good decade?

IGOR: He has had a string of good luck. You cannot plan on something like that.

MATT: You certainly can't.

IGOR: Then again, you had a hit play two years ago. Well, almost a hit play.

MATT: Almost doesn't count in the theatre, Igor. It *has* to count in real life. That's the one major difference between them. (*Pause.*) Maybe you should ask Spencer to read your play.

IGOR: I already try, Matt. But. He is too busy. Anyway, I see your play many times, sir. More times than I can count.

MATT: Well, it couldn't have been *that* many, it only ran about six weeks . . .

IGOR: As long as it ran, I saw it, Matt Ableman.

MATT: You're kidding. How could you afford to?

IGOR: How could I *not* afford to, is the question? After it closed, I had no theatre to clean for another month and a half!

MATT: You . . . cleaned the theatre?

IGOR: Every night, sir, after every performance. The director — pugh! — to tell you the truth, I don't think he did your words justice, that director, I don't know what *you* thought..

MATT: Yes, well, he's a very nice man . . .

IGOR: Where does nice get you in show business, Matt? Hah? You tell me! Where does nice get you *anywhere* in the world? Look at the Jews who were nice when the Nazis came into the ghetto and said, "Okay, now, time to get on the trains to go to the seaside for vacation . . . ." The Jews said, "Thank you, thank you very much . . . "

MATT: (*Uneasy.*) Now, Igor, uh, I really don't think . . .

IGOR: *Nice!* Anyway, Matt, I decided, after seeing your play, that I would try writing something myself, which it has always been a dream of mine to do.

MATT: That's nice, Igor. I mean, *not* nice . . . Listen, I've had a very rough few days . . .

IGOR: Yes, absolutely. I am finished with explanations, you have been most kind. Here is play. You are a good man, Matt. I thank you from the bottom of my heart. Be brutal. Spare no insult. Take no hostages. I must make this my best effort, because I have nothing, I know nobody, and if this play does not succeed, I have no idea what I am going to do with myself . . .

MATT: Oh, now, Mr. Fuchs, er, Igor . . .

IGOR: No, it is true. We are all masters of our circumstance, Matt. Or maybe we are its victims. Who knows? I suppose there are millions of people every day who are learning to accept what is going to happen to them . . . You never know what you can live with, until you have to live with it . . . Do you, Matt . . .

MATT: What . . . ? No . . . I don't suppose you do.

(Igor exits. Matt stands for a moment.)

I don't suppose you do..

THE INNOCENT'S CRUSADE
by Keith Reddin

Dramatic / 2 Men
> Bill: a young man trying to plan his future, 18
> Karl: his hardworking father, 50s

The Setting: a roadside motel, poolside, the present

While on a road trip to visit colleges, Bill and Karl argue by the pool at two in the morning.

O   O   O

BILL: Hey, Dad . . .
KARL: What?
BILL: What are you doing out here?
KARL: What? Who is that?
BILL: It's Bill. Hey, Dad, it's like 2 in the morning.
KARL: So.
BILL: So, you should be . . . you got to drive in the morning. We got to go to the next school.
KARL: I know. You think I don't know that? What's the matter with you?
BILL: Nothing. It's just you were passed out here by the pool.
KARL: I wasn't passed out.
BILL: You were. What if you fell into the pool or something?
KARL: I'm not in the pool, I'm in this chair.
BILL: But you could of slipped off, you could have slipped right off the chair into the pool and drowned maybe. Or somebody could have come up behind your chair and dipped your chair, just tilted it a little and you would fall into the water and you'd never know it, you would be dead and never know it.
KARL: What are you talking about?
BILL: Somebody could have killed you easily. You'd never know.
KARL: Who's going to kill me, what are . . .
BILL: Could be anybody. They don't even have to know you. It could be a complete stranger. They might just be walking by and see you knocked out in the chair and slide you into that

pool and we'd find you in the water face down, your face all bloated. Stiff as a board. Eyes bugging out. How do you think Mom would like that?

KARL: What the hell are you doing out at this time of the night?

BILL: I was taking a walk, I was thinking about taking a swim, I thought a swim would be kind of wild now, nobody awake, just me alone at the pool, and I come over here and you're out cold.

KARL: You don't have a swimsuit on.

BILL: Underneath. I have my bathing trunks on underneath my usual clothes. I was making sure nobody was out here for my nocturnal laps and then what do I find, but my dad sitting here. How many of those beers you had?

KARL: I'm fine.

BILL: I'm sure you're fine. I asked you . . .

KARL: I know what you asked. I'm getting up now. (*He tries to get up. Pause.*) Go back to your room.

BILL: Maybe I should help you . . .

KARL: I don't need your help. I need your help I'll ask you, but I don't need any help from you, you can't do anything, you're not going to get into a top school, you know why?

BILL: Why, Dad?

KARL: You screw up all the things you try. You never see them through, you give up.

BILL: Come on . . .

KARL: I'M TELLING YOU SOMETHING, LISTEN! (*Pause.*)

BILL: I'm listening.

KARL: Those lessons. Those music lessons. You can't play the piano, you don't have any talent, I told your mother that, you don't have the talent or the drive or the ability to learn to play the piano or any musical instrument because you're a . . . I'm the one with the talent. Me. I tell people if I had the chance I could of . . . but I didn't have the time for that . . . I didn't . . .

BILL: I know you had to work hard.

KARL: You're right I had to work hard, you don't know . . . you never finish anything. Then when you mess up, you lie about it.

BILL: I don't.

KARL: Uh huh. Where are you going. I'm talking to you.

BILL: I'm still here.

KARL: Because I'm talking to you.

BILL: Come on Dad, let's not talk anymore. (*Pause*.) Let's go to bed . . . People are turning on their lights.

KARL: I know when it's time to go to bed. It's time to go to bed.

JEFFREY
by Paul Rudnick

Serio-Comic / 2 Men
   Jeffrey: a gay man determined to give up sex, 20-30
   Steve: in love with Jeffrey, HIV-positive, 20-30

The Setting: St. Vincent's Hospital, NYC, the present

When Jeffrey goes to the hospital for a blood test, he runs into Steve, a man to whom he is terribly attracted, but whose HIV-positive status keeps him at bay.

O   O   O

JEFFREY: Are you following me?
STEVE: Of course. I always follow men into clinics.
JEFFREY: How are you?
STEVE: Still positive. Darn.
JEFFREY: Okay . . .
STEVE: And you? What brings you to St. Vincent's high-profile outpatient facility? White sale?
JEFFREY: Blood test.
   (*Steve grins and crosses his fingers, on both hands.*)
STEVE: I'm sorry. There was one thing I never told you. I'm HIV-positive. And obnoxious.
JEFFREY: I knew.
STEVE: Still no acting work?
JEFFREY: No.
STEVE: Still no day job?
JEFFREY: No.
STEVE: Still no sex?
JEFFREY: Steve.
STEVE: You know, Jeffrey, St. Vincent's is not just another Blue Cross pavilion and biopsy barn. Oh no.
JEFFREY: What is with you?
STEVE: Oh, I don't know. Being here, in my living room, and seeing you – it's a killer combo. It's just got me all a-tingle. What shall I wear?

(*Steve goes to the medical cart, and begins holding up various items. His tone is that of a haughty, scintillating host at a fashion show.*)

STEVE: What will today's sassy and sophisticated HIV-positive male be wearing this spring, to tempt the elusive, possibly negative wait-person? Let's begin with the basics – a gown! (*With a flourish, he unfurls a green hospital gown and puts it on over his clothes.*)

It's crisp, it's cotton, it's been sterilized over 5,000 times – it always works.

(*He begins to model the gown, as if on a runway.*)

It's a go-nowhere, do-nothing look, with a peek-a-boo rear and a perky plasma accent. Add pearls and pentamidine, and you're ready for remission.

JEFFREY: Only in green?

STEVE: Please! Green is the navy blue of health care. But it's the accessories that really make the man. Earrings . . .

(*He holds two syringes up to his ears and aims them at Jeffrey.*)

Careful! Hat . . .

(*He places a bedpan on his head, as a chapeau; he removes the bedpan and reads the label.*)

"Sani-care!" And of course . . .

(*He holds up two surgical gloves.*)

Gloves!

JEFFREY: (*Very entertained, applauding.*) I'll take it.

STEVE: Cash or charge?

(*He pretends to take a charge card from Jeffrey.*)

Oh no – but according to this, Madam is HIV-negative. This is not for you. This is only for a select few, the truly chic, the fashion plates who may not live to see the fall collections.

JEFFREY: Steve . . .

STEVE: Can I show you something in – a healthy person? Someone without complications? Someone you could bear to touch?

JEFFREY: Look . . .

STEVE: Okay. Okay. Show's over.

(*He curtsies.*)

Merci.

JEFFREY: Are you all right?

STEVE: (*Tugging off the gown.*) What do you care? Stop being so compassionate. No one's watching.

JEFFREY: Jesus Christ!

STEVE: I'm sorry, I'm a little manic today. And I didn't expect to see you here. I'm being a jerk.

JEFFREY: No, you're fine. I admire your spirit. And your humor.

STEVE: Don't admire me! Fuck me! Admiration gets me an empty dancecard, except for the chest x-rays and the occasional march on Washington. Admiration gets me a lovely memorial and a square on the quilt!

NURSE'S VOICE ON PA SYSTEM: Jeffrey Calloway to examining room one, Jeffrey Calloway.

STEVE: Your table is ready.

JEFFREY: Do you want to go first?

STEVE: Why?

JEFFREY: I don't mind.

STEVE: Jeffrey, I am not here to see the doctor. Surprise!

JEFFREY: You're not?

STEVE: No, I'm on my way to the tenth floor, to see the AIDS babies.

JEFFREY: What?

STEVE: As a volunteer. The last time I was up there, there were eight. They were all abandoned, or their parents had died. And no one would touch them, the nurses were all scared, or busy. The first baby I saw was just lying there, staring, not even crying. But when I held her, she finally smiled and gurgled and acted like a baby. We're all AIDS babies, Jeffrey. And I don't want to die without being held.

THE LINE THAT PICKED UP 1000 BABES (AND HOW IT CAN WORK FOR YOU)
by Eric Berlin

Serio-Comic / 2 Men
  Alan & Benny: two guys cruising a singles bar, 20-30

The Setting: a singles bar

Benny has recently purchased a book on how to pick up "babes." Here, he shares some of his new-found knowledge with a skeptical Alan.

O   O   O

ALAN: This place is a goddamn meat market.
BENNY: People meet people, that's all.
ALAN: That's all.
BENNY: They have to. You're here, too, don't forget.
ALAN: I'm here being me.
BENNY: What's that mean?
ALAN: Being *me*. You're here being whoever happens to be popular at the time. What that *book* says.
BENNY: Man, forget the book, can't you?
ALAN: No. I can't. It's too stupid to just forget.
BENNY: Well, try. (*Man.*)
ALAN: I have a couple of questions.
BENNY: About the book?
ALAN: Yes. Okay? Then I'll back off.
BENNY: Bullshit.
ALAN: Just listen.
BENNY: What?
ALAN: Okay. Question Number One. If there's *one line* that's picked up a thousand babes, like it says, then why is that book two hundred pages long?
BENNY: Well, hell. What you don't know. There's more to it than just the line. There's more. You have to say it the right way. There's a *way* to say the line . . . You have to say it to the right *girl*. You –

ALAN: The right girl?

BENNY: Yes.

ALAN: Okay. (*Pause. Alan stifles a grin.*) No, go on, what?

BENNY: What's the matter with that? Stop putting down what you don't know about, huh? You can't say the line to just anybody. You can't try to pick up some ninety-year-old lady.

ALAN: Is that what the book said or did you figure that out by yourself?

BENNY: There's a long chapter as to who the right girl is.

ALAN: You mean "babe."

BENNY: Yeah, girl, babe, whatever.

ALAN: Which leads me to my second question. I've always wanted to ask this. What the hell is a "babe"?

BENNY: A girl, you moron.

ALAN: You see? When was that book written? Nobody calls girls "babes" anymore.

BENNY: Oh no?

ALAN: *Do* they?

BENNY: You don't call them babes to their faces. Unless you're trying to make some *point* –

ALAN: Oh, behind their *backs*! I get it.

BENNY: Alan: It's just the same thing. Babes are girls. The guidelines in this book –

ALAN: Are time-tested, I know, you told me.

BENNY: It was written in the seventies. Babes then are girls now.

ALAN: But not every girl is a babe.

BENNY: No.

ALAN: The book says that.

BENNY: Right.

ALAN: A very specific type of girl. Less than ninety, for one thing.

BENNY: Yes.

ALAN: Say, eighty-six, eighty-seven . . .

BENNY: Now, look –

ALAN: So where do you draw the line? Are there forty-year-old babes out there?

BENNY: Don't use the book, Okay? Don't even listen to me. All right? But what I'm saying: This book has been time-tested. It works.

ALAN: Actually, I hear that some girls don't even like to be called *girls* now. They're *women*.

BENNY: That is the worst kind of girl.

ALAN: You mean, girls who think. Girls who think are automatically out.

BENNY: They can think, I don't care.

ALAN: They just can't think a *lot*. Does that book give you tips on how to talk about current events?

BENNY: Current events? Who talks about current events in a bar like this?

ALAN: How'd the authors of that book know you'd be *coming* to a bar like this?

BENNY: They said to.

ALAN: Which brings me to my third question: Why would you take a handbook for picking up girls to the bar you plan on patronizing? Wouldn't it be a better idea to just read it and leave it home? You don't want the girls here to *know* you're using a book, now, do you?

BENNY: I have it in my coat pocket. It's a pocket-sized book. They'll never know I have it. If I have to read it, I'll go into the men's room.

ALAN: What if it falls out? You're having a drink with this girl – this *babe* – and you've used the great "line" and a couple of pretty good back-up lines, and then she tells a really funny joke. And you laugh so hard that you almost fall over backwards, but you get your balance back, but out of your coat pocket falls this *book*. Naturally it falls face up, so the title is readable by everyone in the room, so everyone knows you're using a handbook to pick up girls. And once they know that, no girl on the planet will ever speak to you again.

BENNY: That won't happen.

ALAN: Why's that, babes can't tell jokes, either?

BENNY: I mean the book won't fall out.

ALAN: Oooookay. Now. About this *babe* business. Show me a babe.

BENNY: Let's see . . . her. Over there.

ALAN: Where?

BENNY: By the jukebox.

ALAN: Looking in at it?

BENNY: Yeah.

ALAN: How can you tell? She's not even facing this direction. You don't even know what she looks like.

BENNY: You don't need to know what she looks like.

ALAN: Then what the hell are you going by?

BENNY: Look at the way she's dressed. Tight blue jeans is the first thing talked about in Chapter Three.

ALAN: Chapter Three?

BENNY: Chapter Three: "What is a Babe?"

ALAN: There – *wait.* There she is. Okay, now you see what she looks like. Is she a babe?

BENNY: Yes. Definitely.

ALAN: Why? What seals it?

BENNY: The make-up.

ALAN: She's wearing too much. I see her face and I *still* don't know what she looks like.

BENNY: That's just it. Too much make-up is a sure sign.

ALAN: A sure sign. Of . . . babeness.

BENNY: Call them what you will.

ALAN: But, now, wait, do you *like* girls with too much make-up?

BENNY: I can take them or leave them.

ALAN: Or take them and then leave them.

BENNY: Now that's not fair.

ALAN: Okay, sorry . . . so are you going to do something about her?

BENNY: I don't know, maybe. Maybe.

ONE-EYED VENUS AND THE BROTHERS
by Le Wilhelm

Serio-Comic / 2 Men
Rufus: a devoted fisherman, 30-40
Ron: his handicapped younger brother, 18

The Setting: the bank of the James River, Missouri Ozarks, 1959

Rufus has decided that Ron should lose his virginity in order to feel more like a man. Here, Rufus outlines this notion to a surprised Ron.

O   O   O

RUFUS: Don't think Ralph'll be going to Californie.
RON: Huh?
RUFUS: Ralph won't be going to Californie.
RON: Course he's going, Rufus. Nothing here for him.
RUFUS: Not much . . . just some graves up at the cemetery, this here river, you and me. That's all.
RON: Be here if he wants to come back.
RUFUS: This ol' river could dry up. You and me, we might head for Lord knows where. Not got much here, but when it's all you got, hard to leave it. I know.
RON: That why you ain't going to Californie?
RUFUS: Yeah. That and Patch.
RON: Like her, don't you?
RUFUS: Yeah. She likes me too, Good woman. Should've married her. Might have if she hadn't gone off to college. 'Fraid she'd be too high falutin' for –
RON: You going to be afraid of me when I go away to college and come back here?
RUFUS: You're my kin. That's different.
RON: Mmmh?
RUFUS: Maybe it ain't, but I married a good woman. Shirley was the best. And she's the kind you're supposed to marry.
RON: Mmmh. (*Pause.*) If I ever get married, I'll marry the one I

love.

RUFUS: Probably the best idea.

RON: Mmmh.

RUFUS: Ron.

RON: Mmmh?

RUFUS: Need to speak to you about something.

RON: Yeah.

RUFUS: It's time you got a piece of nook.

RON: Huh?

RUFUS: Nookie. (*Ron is slightly shocked.*) It's time you got a piece. Don't you think?

RON: (*Embarrassed.*) I guess.

RUFUS: It is. You're eighteen. I was seventeen my first. Do wonders for you, boy. Change your whole life. Make you a man.

RON: (*Laughing shyly.*) Woman'll do that for me?

RUFUS: Not a woman. Nookie.

RON: Oh.

RUFUS: Yeah. Seen it happen many a time. Boy gets a little, next day he's a man. Roger, when he got his first piece, you wouldn't have believed the change. I know he's still kinda goofy acting, but you don't remember him before, you's too young. He was an embarrassment to the family. And you need a piece, Ron. Time. Past time.

RON: So I won't be an embarrassment to the family?

RUFUS: No. You ain't that now. Now, do girls like you?

RON: Yeah. Actually, Rufus –

RUFUS: You got a lot to offer them, you know.

RON: Huh?

RUFUS: You do. Now, you having polio might make a difference to some of them. You being crippled. But you make up for it in other areas.

RON: 'Cause I make good grades?

RUFUS: (*Laughing.*) Hell, no. I'm talking 'bout your lizard.

RON: Huh?

RUFUS: You got a big lizard, boy. Bigger than mine. One of the biggest I ever saw. Woman like big lizards, boy. Least most of them do. Some of 'em say they like to reach for it. (*Laughs.*) I've been told that a couple of times, but I 'spect they's lying.

RON: Mmmh.

RUFUS: They'll say it don't make a difference, that they don't think about it. Bunk. They like big lizards. And you got a big lizard. (*Laughing.*) I couldn't believe it when I walked out behind the barn and caught you –

RON: Rufus.

RUFUS: No need to be embarrassed. All men do it.

RON: Not supposed to.

RUFUS: All men do it. Since Shirley died, if I didn't, I'd go nuts.

RON: Well, at church they say it's –

RUFUS: You can't pay much attention to that stuff, Ron. I figure when the Good Book talks about spilling seed, it ain't even talking to us now. It meant them people back then, because they needed lots of kids for the tribe to survive. But we got plenty of young'n's now, so it's okay to spill your seed if you want. Actually, I figure it's mostly women who want to say it ain't right to be playing with yourself.

RON: Huh?

RUFUS: Women are jealous.

RON: Huh?

RUFUS: They don't want us doing it with ourselves. They want us doing it with them. So they like to make a big thing out of spilling your seed making God mad. Only reason they do that is because they just can't stand the thought of you doing it by yourself and them not getting any pleasure out of it. See?

RON: Uh huh.

RUFUS: You don't need to be embarrassed by what I seen, not at all.

RON: Mmmh. Let's not talk about it anymore, okay?

RUFUS: Sure, we got to talk about tonight. About you getting your first woman.

RON: Huh?

RUFUS: Tonight might be your night. Might be your night to have the best.

RON: Who? (*Rufus looks at him and smiles.*) Patch?

RUFUS: Patch.

RON: She's. . .

RUFUS: Huh?

RON: Kinda old.

RUFUS: She ain't that old, boy. And she's experienced. She'll be gentle with you, teach you. I'm not saying she's going to offer, but, boy, if she does, you count yourself one lucky man. It'd mean that you'd start with the best there is.

RON: Rufus, I –

RUFUS: This is awful important to me. I'm kinda glad you haven't been with anyone before. If Patch wants to . . . it'd be . . . Patch and I loved one another, but . . . You see, Ron, Patch is something that I shared with Roger and Ralph. She's their first as well as mine, and if she was yours, too. It'd be a family . . .

RON: I –

RUFUS: Nice looking woman, don't you think?

RON: Mmmh.

RUFUS: And she's smart like you, Ron, got herself an education. Just like you're going to do.

RON: Mmmh.

RUFUS: Good, it's set. Sure hope she's in the mood.

RON: Yeah.

RUFUS: Stars coming out, going to be a beautiful night. There's the big dipper.

RON: Hope the moon don't shine down too bright. Keep the fish from biting. I'd sure like to catch a big mess of fish for the pie supper tomorrow night.

RUFUS: Don't know how many we'll catch, but we'll catch a few, Ron. Always do. Just got to leave it up to the old river. Whatever it wants to offer, that's what you take.

SOMEONE WHO'LL WATCH OVER ME
by Frank McGuinness

Dramatic / 2 Men
 Edward: An Irishman held hostage in Lebanon, 30-40
 Michael: his British cellmate, 30-40

The Setting: a cell in Lebanon, the present

Edward and Michael have been held hostage in Lebanon for months. When Adam, their American cellmate, is executed, they react with fear and grief.

O   O   O

MICHAEL: Adam is dead, Edward.

EDWARD: You want him dead. You feel safer with him dead. One of us down, and no more to go. With him dead there'll be a big outcry and we will be saved. Isn't that it? Well, listen, get that out of your head, for if they've put him down, they can put us down as well. Dogs together, to be shot. Take no consolation from imagining him dead. It won't save you. It won't save me.

MICHAEL: No it won't save you. You hope it might save you, but you're perfectly correct, his death won't save you. You condemn yourself out of your own mouth. It isn't me who wants him dead. It's you, isn't it?
 (*Silence.*)
 I don't blame you for thinking that. You want to give his death some – some sense of sacrifice. You are in grief, in mourning. And you are mad with grief.

EDWARD: He is not –

MICHAEL: (*Roars.*) Dead, he is, and you know it.

EDWARD: You know nothing.

MICHAEL: I know about grief. About mourning. How it can destroy you. I know.
 (*Silence.*)
 You know he's dead, don't you?
 (*Silence.*)

Say it, he is dead.
(*Silence.*)

EDWARD: He died. I needed him. Jesus, I needed him.
(*Silence.*)

How could he leave me? How could he do this? Without him, how will I get through this?

MICHAEL: Bury him.
(*Silence.*)

Remember him.
(*Silence.*)

What was he like?

EDWARD: He was gentle. He was kind. He could be cruel, when he was afraid, and while he was often afraid, as we all are afraid, he was not often cruel. He was brave, he could protect himself, and me, and you. He was beautiful to look at. I watched him as he slept one night I couldn't sleep. He moved that night through his sleep like a man not dreaming of what life had in store for him. He was innocent. Kind, gentle. Friend. I believe it goes without saying, love, so I never said. He is dead. Bury him. Perpetual light shine upon him. May his soul rest in peace. Amen.
(*Silence.*)

MICHAEL: Love bade me welcome; yet my soul drew back,
    Guiltie of dust and sinne.
    But quick-ey'd Love, observing me grow slack
    From my first entrance in,
    Drew nearer to me, sweetly questioning,
    If I lack'd anything.

    A guest, I answer'd, worthy to be here:
    Love said, You shall be he.
    I the unkinde, ungratefull? Ah my deare,
    I cannot look on thee.
    Love took my hand, and smiling did reply,
    Who made the eyes but I?

    Truth Lord, but I have marr'd them: Let my shame
    Go where it doth deserve.
    And know you not, sayes Love, who bore the blame?
    My deare, then I will serve.

You must sit down, sayes Love, and taste my meat:
So I did sit and eat.
(*Silence.*)
EDWARD: I'm hungry.
MICHAEL: Then eat.
EDWARD: Dear friend.
(*Edward eats.*)
He's dead.
MICHAEL: We are not.
(*Lights fade.*)

Permissions

for charity or gain and whether or not admission is charged.

Stock royalty quoted on application to Samuel French, Inc.

For all other right than those stipulated above, apply to Robert Lantz, The Lantz Office, 888 Seventh Avenue, New York, NY 10106-0084.